T0390070

"Your humble light,
the fire of your mind blinds you:
If you walk with a lantern in the dark,
you won't see the stars."

—*Hans Børli*

Susan Redman

LOVE SHACKS

Romantic cabin charmers, modern getaways
and rustic retreats around the world

images
Publishing

INTRODUCTION

The great delights of escaping urban life to commune with nature in a stylish bolthole hidden in a remote or rural setting is best shared with others. Time away with loved ones can strengthen the bonds of precious relationships. And since the focus is on relaxing and getting out and about together, couples, families and friends can truly disconnect from the pressures of their busy city lives.

So why do we yearn to skip town to our own little holiday house with those we love? Is it merely to reconnect, reassess and reset our lives? What influence does a nature environment have on the experience? To what extent do people and places inspire the design of holiday homes? And, finally, is this desire for 'slow living' universally held across all nationalities?

Love Shacks explores this 'desire' from the perspective of holiday homeowners throughout the world who, in telling their personal stories, provide answers. Hailing from Europe, Scandinavia, the Americas, Asia, Australia and New Zealand, their experiences outline remarkably similar aspirations and endeavours, and all are focused on creating a life unhurried—however temporary—in a home away from home.

Featuring twenty-three beautiful properties, from architecturally sublime modern escapes and restored rustic retreats to cool cabins and charming cottages, *Love Shacks* also reveals what design elements have been important to homeowners in realising their dream holiday home. Since most of the 'love shacks' are owned by 'creatives', their imagination and enterprise is clearly evident in the designs. Some holiday-homeowners have collaborated with architects to achieve their vision, while others have worked tirelessly to restore and renovate dilapidated structures left unloved and in disrepair.

The book is divided into three sections based on each property's architectural type of either charmer, modern or rustic. These sections are filled with chapters, which each feature the getaway house of one couple or family. Their narratives are illustrated with lavish photographs of the getaway, inside and out, their loved ones, and the stunning surroundings in which the properties are located. Additionally, these pages feature a 'travel' aspect in the form of 'wild notes' at the end of each chapter.

In essence, *Love Shacks* gets to the 'heart' of the holiday home design trend by providing authentic first-person accounts and photography to picture what stylish, slow-living getaway homes mean to those people across the globe with the creative vision and deep desire to reconnect with nature and with each other. Whether the house is built at considerable expense, passed down through generations, acquired by cultural tradition or bought for a song, these 'shacks' are architectural odes to an unhurried life, to their natural surroundings and, ultimately, to love.

—Susan Redman

"What could be more romantic than watching the sun rise and set or stargazing at night from a stylish little getaway in the wilderness with the ones you love?"

THE CHARMERS

These cool cabins, charming cottages and salty sea shacks, nestled in woods, on mountains and along the coast, offer both nature lovers and adventure seekers the chance to explore. Some are designed from scratch, others are rehabilitated, but all bring a sense of the great outdoors inside by incorporating big windows and featuring reclaimed materials. Their cosy but stylish interiors boast new appliances while sheltering inhabitants from cold weather with the inclusion of log fires or saunas. In summer, residents can take a refreshing dip in nearby rivers, lakes or oceans. Life in the wild inspires shack décor, too, evident in colourful vintage or folksy textiles, ornaments and furnishings.

BUSHY SUMMERS MINER'S SHACK

Lettes Bay, Tasmania, Australia

The rugged west coast of Tasmania couldn't be a more remote setting for a stylish little bolthole, but this is exactly where designer Claire Lloyd and artist Matthew Usmar Lauder found the rustic miner's shack that would become their antipodean escape.

Located in a quiet backwater of Macquarie Harbour, the shack is set literally on the edge of tranquil Lettes Bay. "The view from our window is beautiful. You can almost touch the water and jetty out front," says Claire. "It's beyond magical."

The bay is dotted with heritage-listed miners' shacks. Most were erected between 1920 and 1950 and constructed from scraps of tin and anything that could be reclaimed. They were built by men working in the Mount Lyell mines and used as holiday getaways for their families. It was a tough industry in a harsh environment, echoing the harbour's brutal colonial penal history of the early 1800s.

When Claire and Matthew purchased their shack in 2018, it needed a serious makeover. "We worked on the renovations together, Matthew doing the lion's share, with help from a local builder," says Claire. "It was a wonderful project, one which we poured so much love into."

The small shack, christened Bushy Summers, was made sturdy and completely reconfigured to take advantage of the bay view. New, old windows, a stable front door and insulation were installed, and the plumbing and electrics updated. The interiors were stripped back to the original tin walls.

Simplicity and light are important to Claire, who wanted to ensure the shack's interiors followed her vision to create a bright living space. "Whenever I do a project there are huge lashings of white paint involved, so the interiors are white. It's always been my thing."

Textures are important, too. Carved wooden doors frame the entry to the bathroom. A shell light hanging in the bedroom casts pretty shadows across the ceiling. There is linen bedding, velvet cushions, and hand-made ceramics.

For artist Matthew, it's all about utilising what's at hand: "Matt is brilliant at making and recycling, so lots of the furniture was made from scraps or found objects," says Claire. "For example, he made our table from an old door he found under the front deck. He also paints landscapes and draws the resident ducks, ravens and cockatoos. I turned these drawings into linen cushion covers, tea towels and aprons."

Claire grew up in Sydney, and still has an apartment in the city, but spent much of her adult life as a creative director in London for various design and advertising agencies. She's also an author of two books, *Sensual Living* and *My Greek Island Home*.

Claire met Matthew in London: "Matthew is an extremely talented artist and has recently turned his hand to building Bushy Summers and did a fine job—and we are never short of one of his beautiful paintings to hang on the walls."

Having left London behind, the couple now live between Sydney, Tasmania, and the Greek island of Lesvos in the northeastern Aegean, where they own another getaway. "We usually split our time 50/50 between the southern and northern hemispheres, following the summer!" says Claire.

Since the shack is only 36 square metres (387.5 square feet), visiting friends and family stay nearby. However, Claire says they can soon holiday together as she and Matthew have started work on a 'big sister' for Bushy Summers, called Rosy Summers. (See page 284 for rental details.)

"It was a wonderful project, one which we poured so much love into. Simplicity and light were important to me and for Matthew it was collecting and making—the style and interiors of the shack reflect that combination."

—*Claire*

"Some evenings in the summer when the sun doesn't set until late, we go to Ocean Beach with a picnic and watch the sea and wonder at its vastness, there is no landmass at this longitude between it and South America."

—*Claire*

Claire and Matthew never tire of walking along the bay or further afield to Hogarth Falls. Some summer evenings they drive to Ocean Beach, a 40-kilometre (25-mile) stretch of soft white sand, about ten minutes away. "We take a picnic and watch the sea and wonder at its vastness; there is no landmass at this longitude between Tasmania and South America."

Back at home base, there's always a gaggle of resident ducks to feed, "who have no problem letting you know they're hungry," says Claire. Cooking and "drinking delicious Tassie wine" is always on the agenda. The couple love eating lobster when available, sourcing local fresh eggs, enjoying homemade jams and chutneys, and occasionally purchasing home-grown produce from roadside stalls.

"Being at Bushy Summers is such a chill-out from city life, and there is no better place to do that than on our deck with its fabulous bay view," says Claire. "The hues change through the day from blue to pink. It's heavenly."

"There is inspiration from every window, in fact the windows act as frames turning the external views into ever-changing paintings, with the quacking of the ducks and local birdsong as the soundtrack."

—Claire

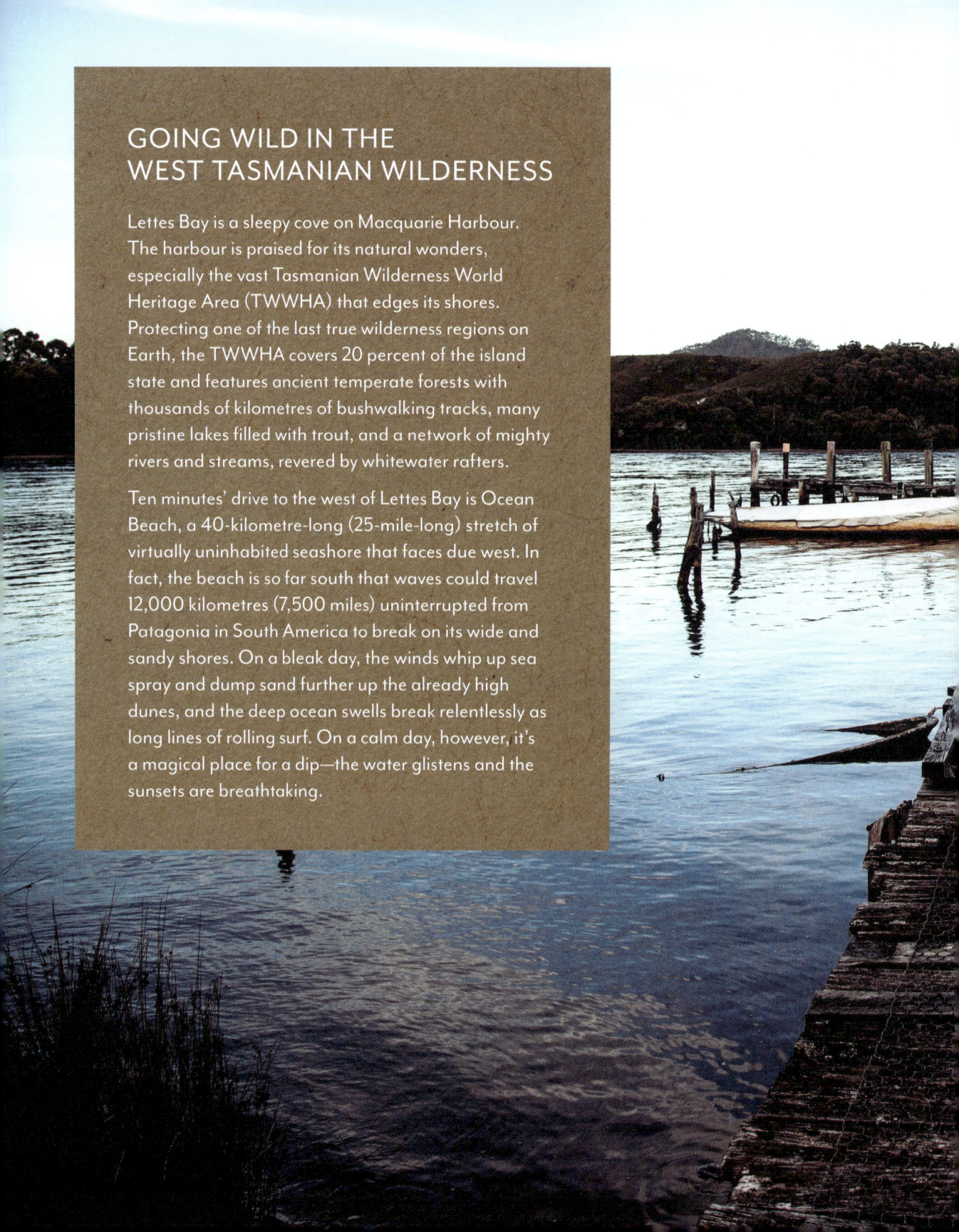

GOING WILD IN THE WEST TASMANIAN WILDERNESS

Lettes Bay is a sleepy cove on Macquarie Harbour. The harbour is praised for its natural wonders, especially the vast Tasmanian Wilderness World Heritage Area (TWWHA) that edges its shores. Protecting one of the last true wilderness regions on Earth, the TWWHA covers 20 percent of the island state and features ancient temperate forests with thousands of kilometres of bushwalking tracks, many pristine lakes filled with trout, and a network of mighty rivers and streams, revered by whitewater rafters.

Ten minutes' drive to the west of Lettes Bay is Ocean Beach, a 40-kilometre-long (25-mile-long) stretch of virtually uninhabited seashore that faces due west. In fact, the beach is so far south that waves could travel 12,000 kilometres (7,500 miles) uninterrupted from Patagonia in South America to break on its wide and sandy shores. On a bleak day, the winds whip up sea spray and dump sand further up the already high dunes, and the deep ocean swells break relentlessly as long lines of rolling surf. On a calm day, however, it's a magical place for a dip—the water glistens and the sunsets are breathtaking.

LOVE & MUTINY
BEACH SHACK

Chinaman Wells, Yorke Peninsula, South Australia

It is rare to find an original 1950s Aussie beach shack for sale these days, especially on the beachfront. So when sisters Emma Read and Sarah Hall found one just over two hours' drive from their hometown, near Adelaide, South Australia, they were tickled pink.

The sisters inspected the west-facing house late in the afternoon, when the lemon sun was just setting into pastel pink and mauve hues on the sea's far horizon, strengthening the sisters' romantic connection to the house. "Once we knew the shack only had one owner for most of its life and was painted pink in the 1950s, we were emotionally invested," says Emma.

Sitting high on the beachfront with 360-degree views, the shack is deceptively small, with only two bedrooms and one central living space, a front yard on the sand and a backyard that abuts native scrub. It's located in Chinaman Wells, a tiny coastal and fishing community on the Yorke Peninsula, which is dotted with original Australian beach shacks.

Fishermen say the striking pink house, now repainted in its original hue, serves as a landmark for local seafarers. The coastal foreshores of the Spencer Gulf out front are flat and tidal and ultimately connect to the Great Southern Ocean. "From the house you see and hear pelicans and black swans, as well as native birdlife," says Sarah. "Crabbing and fishing are traditional pastimes here. When we're here, we feel like we we're in another world; we can disconnect."

The sisters called the shack Love & Mutiny, with good reason: "We both left our regular jobs within six months of the purchase, and only continued with our vintage bespoke styling business, Read and Hall," says Sarah. "We felt like it was time to go out on a limb, so we staged a mutiny on our work priorities with the intention to only love what we do for a living. It's created a very appropriate name!"

To update the house, the siblings combined resources, recruiting their two families to help on weekends. "Trades were scarce in this remote location, and we were on a budget, so we took our time through COVID-19 lockdowns and are proud of the result," says Emma.

"When it came to Love & Mutiny, it certainly wasn't going to be a traditional-looking beach house with coastal décor and white walls," says Sarah. "For us, the house told another story, and so in updating and decorating it, we wanted to honour its vibrance and history."

Aesthetically, the sisters drew inspiration from the Bloomsbury period and their mother's interest in clairvoyance. "The house has a celestial and astrological vibe," says Emma. "Come nightfall, it's like being untethered from life, watching the moon rise over the ocean, sitting by the firepit on the beach and stargazing. It connects you to a primitive part of yourself. The house is us from beginning to end, styled entirely from our imagination."

"We chose warm tones to paint the walls to reflect the golden light that floods the shack every morning and evening."

—*Sarah*

"The house has a celestial and astrological vibe. Come nightfall, watching the moon rise over the ocean, it's like being untethered from life."

—*Emma*

To bring that delight to the interiors, the sisters painted the walls in dusty pink and Sundance yellow, colours which seem to accentuate the golden light that bathes the inside of the shack in the late afternoon. They added accents of 1950s-style wallpaper, striped and floral soft furnishings, installed etched midcentury porthole windows in the bathroom, lined the kitchen splashback in tiles decorated with tiny boats, hung original colourful prints on the walls and set up a cocktail cabinet and vintage record player with a curated playlist. For outdoor pleasure, they festooned the large balcony in lights and set a firepit out front in the sand for impromptu sundowner parties.

"There's nothing like seeing the sunrise from the daybed, under a blanket, drinking a hot cup of tea or, at the end of the day, watching the sun set into the sea from the balcony with a cocktail in hand," says Sarah.

The sisters both enjoy an afternoon nap, always waking up to the tidal beach view, and enjoying the quietness and stillness often absent from their regular lives. They also share the experience by renting the house out (see page 284 for details).

Sarah and Emma usually head to the shack with family or friends. Once there, they rarely want to leave. "Reading, listening to music, walking along the beach, yoga on the balcony, sitting by the wood fire, napping—it's a place of quiet reflection because of the water and sky views from every window," says Emma.

"Sometimes we retreat here solo, and don't see a soul," says Sarah. "The quietness reinvigorates you. There is no television or Wi-Fi, the stars are abundant and the geographical location is so unique. We have uninterrupted views of both the sunrise and sunset from the kitchen table—that's so rare in this world."

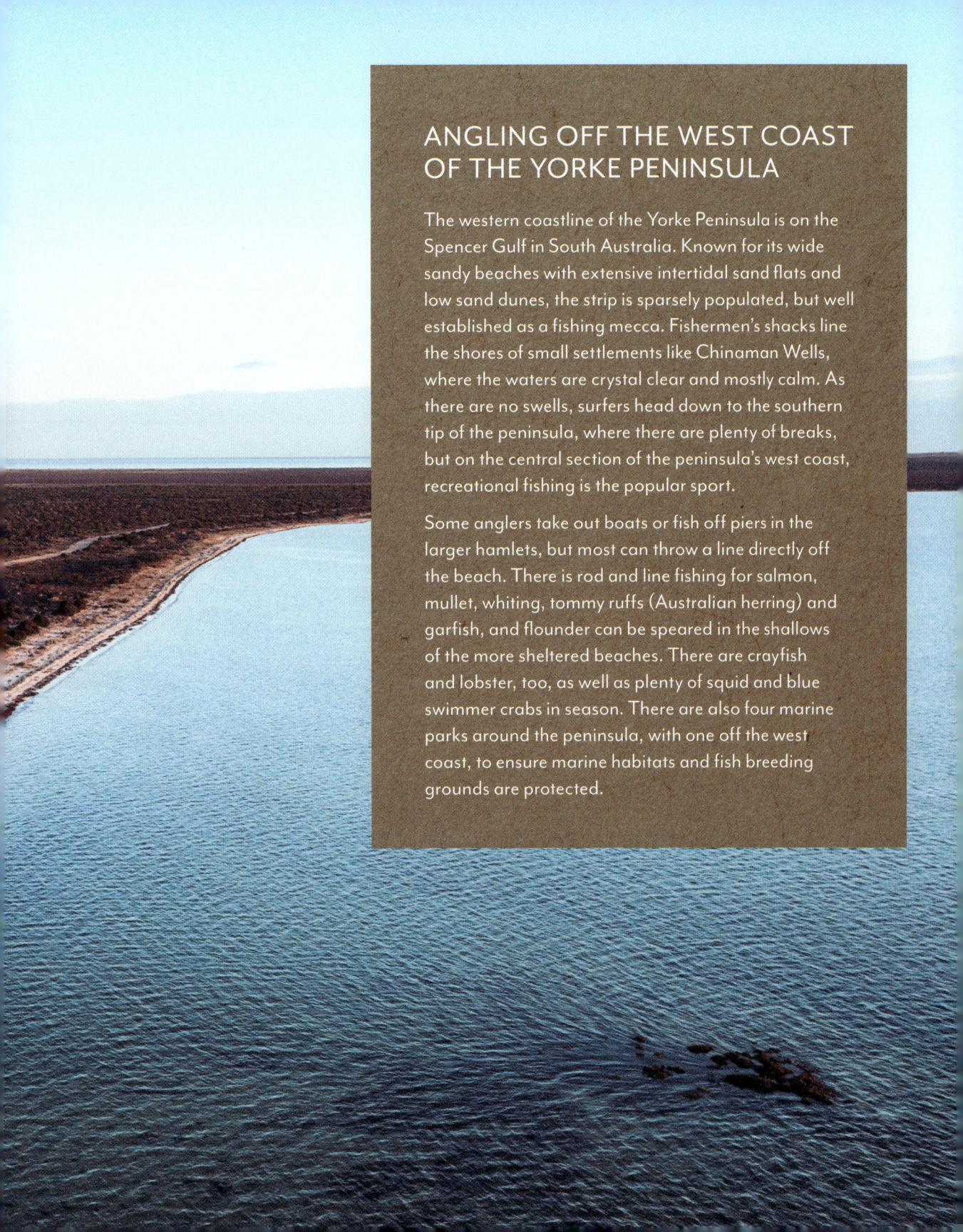

ANGLING OFF THE WEST COAST OF THE YORKE PENINSULA

The western coastline of the Yorke Peninsula is on the Spencer Gulf in South Australia. Known for its wide sandy beaches with extensive intertidal sand flats and low sand dunes, the strip is sparsely populated, but well established as a fishing mecca. Fishermen's shacks line the shores of small settlements like Chinaman Wells, where the waters are crystal clear and mostly calm. As there are no swells, surfers head down to the southern tip of the peninsula, where there are plenty of breaks, but on the central section of the peninsula's west coast, recreational fishing is the popular sport.

Some anglers take out boats or fish off piers in the larger hamlets, but most can throw a line directly off the beach. There is rod and line fishing for salmon, mullet, whiting, tommy ruffs (Australian herring) and garfish, and flounder can be speared in the shallows of the more sheltered beaches. There are crayfish and lobster, too, as well as plenty of squid and blue swimmer crabs in season. There are also four marine parks around the peninsula, with one off the west coast, to ensure marine habitats and fish breeding grounds are protected.

WILD SURF CABIN

Nova Scotia, Canada

An old fisherman's shack on a headland in Nova Scotia offers an expansive view that takes in the wild shores of the Atlantic Ocean. It is here that Canadians Catherine Bernier and partner Gabriel Denis (Cath and Gabe) not only found a refuge to bunker down in during a pandemic lockdown, but a place from where they could reaffirm their connection to the sea.

"Gabe introduced me to his passion for surfing, which has become a shared obsession," says Cath. "All our trips, whether along the Canadian coast or further afield in the Americas, turn into a quest for waves and unique encounters, far from the daily grind."

Cath and Gabe met in Quebec City while Cath was studying psychology and Gabe was launching his own events and marketing business. When the weather warms up, the couple head east to their coastal cabin on a 3-hectare (7-acre) property, which they bought (or as Cath says 'dropped anchor there') in 2018. "It was our dream to own acreage by the sea," says Gabe.

"Nothing is comparable to surfing and the vibe of the Canadian Maritimes," says Cath, even when the water is icy cold, requiring that she and Gabe don full head-to-toe 5-millimetre-thick (¼-inch-thick) wetsuits with booties, gloves and hood! "I grew up in a small coastal fishing village on the remote Gaspésie Peninsula, I need my daily dose of salty sea breeze."

The mornings are sacred at the cabin. "We wake up at first light, stoke the fire, prepare coffee while doing a surf check by surveying the wind and waves conditions out front. We're lucky enough to have a few breaks to choose from. During summer, we drink our coffee outside on the patio. It's the best part of the day."

"After our surf, we love hosting brunch or a barbecue at the cabin with our friends. Sometimes, I harvest sea plants and seaweed from our beach. I really enjoy a fresh salad of beach peas and sea spinach, with apple and quinoa."

As a writer and photographer for the environmentally focused magazine *BESIDE*, Cath uses her creativity "in order to awaken self, collective and environmental awareness", which has resulted in her starting the photography studio, The Parcelles (see page 284 for details), operated from the cabin.

Creativity was also required to initially update the fisherman's shack, which on purchase had no toilet, no electricity, and no water. Gabriel tackled the physical renovations and a new addition, with a little help from mates, while Cath planned interior aesthetics, considering "how design could bridge any gap between beauty, efficiency and sustainability". Transformed over the course of two years, the shack is now the delightfully picturesque and cosy Wild Surf Cabin, boasting a new durable roof and shingles on the outside while inside Cath and Gabe enjoy all the modern conveniences.

To elicit a 'soothing feeling', the cabin's interiors were lined with horizontal planks of pine lightened with a finish of natural Danish whitewash. New windows were installed to bathe the interiors in light. And since the footprint is rather small, a bedroom was tucked into a spacious attic with sturdy ladder access, and a built-in office was located in the hallway.

Just like a chalet has a ski room, the cabin has cleverly incorporated what Cath calls a 'surf closet' to house boards and wetsuits. There is also an essential outdoor shower, and a mud room to clean off after beach treks, as well as an indoor shower so both can get warm after a dip in the chilly Atlantic. "No more fights for the shower!" she says.

"As the cabin used to be a fishing shack, the decoration is mostly an ode to the local fishing lifestyle, such as the old artwork of a sea captain hanging above the dining table," says Cath. "I also collected decorative artefacts from the beach, such as colourful pieces of boat hull, bouquets of dried seaweed and washed fishing ropes, and mixed these with modern artworks and photographs on the wall."

"As the cabin used to be a fishing shack, we wanted to keep the spirit alive, so the decoration is mostly an ode to the local fishing lifestyle, such as the old artwork of a sea captain hanging above the dining table."

—*Catherine*

While the environment is calm in summer, autumn is the couple's favourite season. "The water is still warm but the air is fresh. Trees are changing colours and birds are moving loudly to south, as swells appear to stir our surf desires. We feel really small in our little shack when hurricanes hit the area, but we are stoked as we know good surf will be served. On a stormy night in our attic bedroom, it almost feels like we sleep in a boat. The wind knocks on our door and it's hard to sleep, but our excitement for good surf is high."

This feeling of being rocked by the elements is exactly what Cath and Gabe like about their getaway. Cath says experiencing the forces of nature while sheltering within their little wooden cabin promotes "different connections in our brains and allows me to fully extend my creativity and connect with nature, in all its beauty. It is the entire package that makes our house a special place."

"Nothing is comparable to surfing and the vibe of the Canadian Maritimes. As I grew up by the sea, I need my daily dose of salty breeze. It is where I feel alive the most."

—Catherine

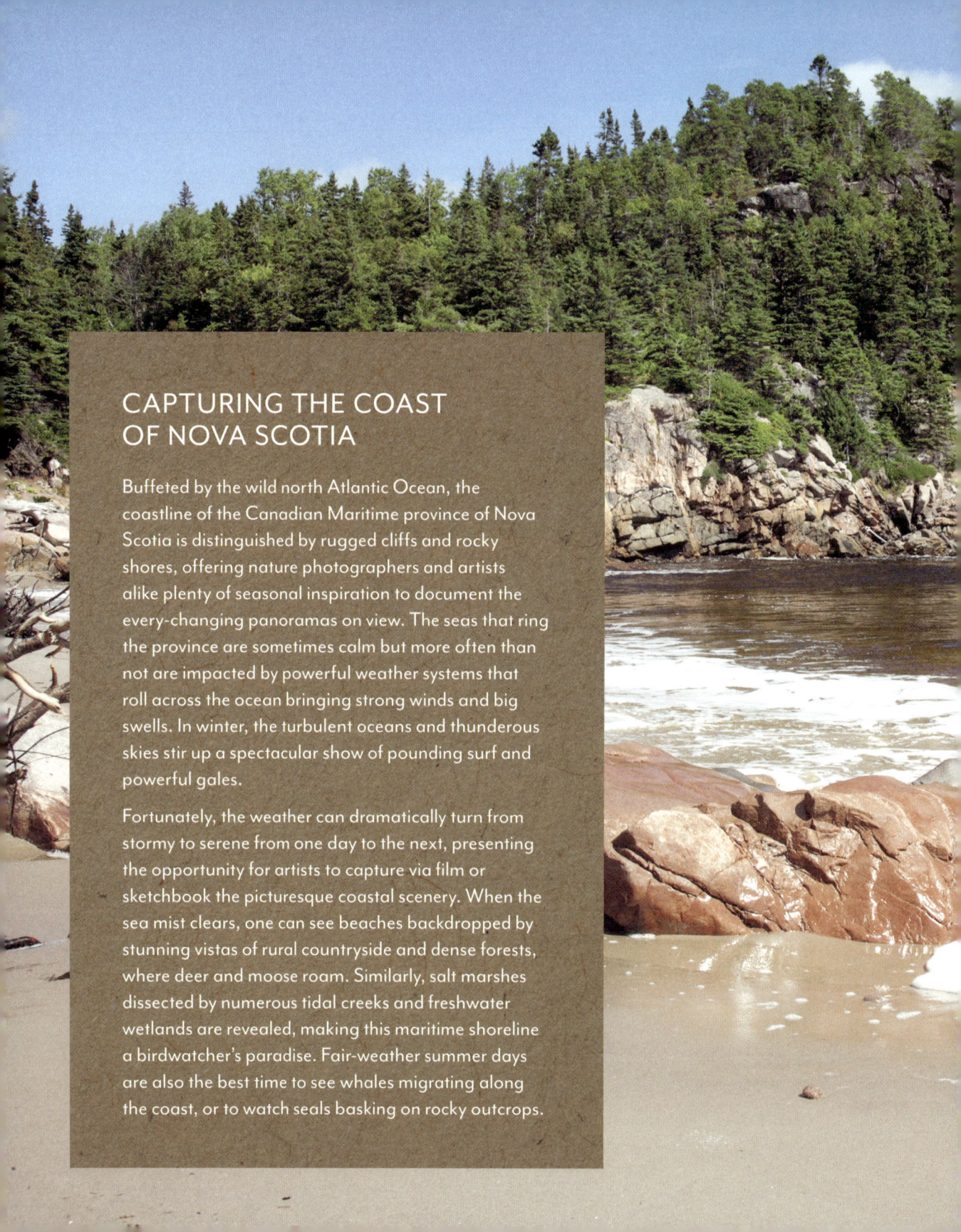

CAPTURING THE COAST OF NOVA SCOTIA

Buffeted by the wild north Atlantic Ocean, the coastline of the Canadian Maritime province of Nova Scotia is distinguished by rugged cliffs and rocky shores, offering nature photographers and artists alike plenty of seasonal inspiration to document the every-changing panoramas on view. The seas that ring the province are sometimes calm but more often than not are impacted by powerful weather systems that roll across the ocean bringing strong winds and big swells. In winter, the turbulent oceans and thunderous skies stir up a spectacular show of pounding surf and powerful gales.

Fortunately, the weather can dramatically turn from stormy to serene from one day to the next, presenting the opportunity for artists to capture via film or sketchbook the picturesque coastal scenery. When the sea mist clears, one can see beaches backdropped by stunning vistas of rural countryside and dense forests, where deer and moose roam. Similarly, salt marshes dissected by numerous tidal creeks and freshwater wetlands are revealed, making this maritime shoreline a birdwatcher's paradise. Fair-weather summer days are also the best time to see whales migrating along the coast, or to watch seals basking on rocky outcrops.

VILLA SYSMÄ

Lake Päijänne, Sysmä, Finland

Finland is known as the land of a thousand lakes. Found dotted around them are *kesämökki* (summer cottages), acquired by city-dwelling Finnish families to tie them to their rural past when life was less complicated. In fact, there are so many *kesämökki* that approximately one in four Finns owns one.

For Johanna and Mikko Haltia, however, three years of looking for a *mökki* that would fulfil their criteria proved unsuccessful. So they took another approach and purchased a 7,800-square-metre (2-acre) parcel of land that featured views of serene Lake Päijänne and Kammiovuori mountain in the distance—a panorama at the top of their wish list.

In 2019 they started to build their perfect getaway. "From the start, it was clear that we needed two buildings, one for us and our young daughter Sophia (five) and one for my sons, Luka (twelve) and Patrik (fourteen)," says Johanna. "We wanted the *mökki* to harmonise with the scenery, and especially the surrounding woodland, so we painted the exteriors a charcoal black."

Johanna and Mikko positioned the structures on the elevated rocky site to face the lake and, in order to enjoy the views from both the living area, the boys' bunkhouse and obligatory sauna, they installed floor-to-ceiling windows. In contrast to the dark exteriors, Johanna and Mikko painted the wood-panelled interiors white, filling the cottages with light.

As the CEO of a large fashion-centric shopping centre in Helsinki, Johanna is surrounded by designer brands all day, so it isn't surprising that she is passionate about style and interiors. "I furnished the *mökki* with items both old and new, practical and vintage." For example, she chose Finnish Artek wall lights, a central Gubi Multi-Lite general light, and installed a practical IKEA kitchen. She also added vintage finds from flea markets such as Arabia-design Finland ceramics for tableware and picked up a set of Vitra wire chairs, which she and Mikko restored and painted for the outdoor dining area.

To keep a small environmental footprint, the couple installed solar panels for the electricity system (the fridge, lights, etc.), and heat the cabin with a wood-burning fireplace, solar-panel heater or a gas-operated heater.

Although the two sleek black cabins are small—the boys' bunkhouse is only 10 square metres (108 square feet) while the main building is 28 square metres (301 square feet), including the essential sauna—the structures are linked by extensive decking. The deck ultimately leads down to a wooden jetty that provides an additional platform for much of the outdoor activities both in and out of the water.

"I furnished the *mökki* with items both old and new, practical and vintage. For example, the kitchen is an IKEA model, with a big porcelain sink. It's stocked with new plates and glasses, but also amazing finds from flea markets such as old Arabia tableware designs."

—*Johanna*

It's no surprise that the large private jetty is the family's favourite hangout. "During summer we have our outdoor 'beds' there," says Johanna. "It's where we sunbathe, jump into the lake to swim, we even do our evening table settings and dinners there, either together or when friends come to visit."

As it takes less than two hours' drive to reach Sysmä, the lake-filled municipality that is north of the family's usual residence in Helsinki, other family members and friends from the city often join Johanna and Mikko. When the couple aren't taking them hiking through the forests or boating out on the lake, they love to cook for everyone. The family even catch their own seafood or collect berries and mushrooms in the surrounding woods to supplement meals.

On most weekends through the warmer months of February through to October, the family heads for the lake. In the morning Mikko takes the kids and their dog to check on the family's fishnets. "Our dog loves to go fishing, she is the first in the boat. Normally we catch some good fish to eat. After cleaning them, we enjoy breakfast together."

In high summer, the kids usually swim all day, play in the sand or sunbathe. Lunch is prepared and then it's time for everyone to take a nap. Energised by a brewed coffee upon awakening, firewood is collected and carried to both the sauna and campfire for burning later.

"On summer evenings, we either steam in the sauna, soak in the hot tub or, since it's light until late, we continue to swim in the lake. In fact, all day and evening, our kids alternate between the sauna, the lake, the hot tub, then back to the lake. We make dinner and eat outside next to the campfire, listening to the sounds of nature and gazing at the beautiful stars."

"During the summer we have our outdoor
'beds' set up on the jetty. It's here that we sunbathe,
jump into the lake, and even enjoy our evening dinners
there with good food, wine and friends."

—*Johanna*

"We love to relax and enjoy the wilderness and silence of Lake Päijänne. It's so safe to swim in the lake, and there is no dangerous wildlife around, despite rare reports of bears and wolves, but we have seen moose and fox in the woods, and falcons in the sky."

—*Johanna*

JUMPING INTO LAKE PÄIJÄNNE

A serene, blue, fresh-water lake edged in thick green pine forest is the quintessential image of Finland. According to Finnish government numbers, there are an astounding 188,000 lakes. The second-largest, and deepest, is Lake Päijänne, which is over 120 kilometres (75 miles) long and is dotted with islands. It's safe to swim, and also provides drinking water to the capital of Helsinki to the south. Technical innovation during the 1960s allowed the clever Finns to tunnel through bedrock for about 120 kilometres (75 miles) to transport the valuable resource to the city.

Red-coloured Stone Age rock paintings are also found around Lake Päijänne. The most common subjects are man, deer, boats and hands. It is thought that the paintings on this lake and others recorded ceremonies or served as signposts for the nomadic tribes that travelled through the lake's landscape, using canoes or dog sleds to cover good distances across the water so as to reduce a hike through rocky forests to the next lake or port of call.

THE BOOKWORM CABIN

Adelin, Mazovia, Poland

Switching off digital devices to catch up on reading has been taken to the next level in this bespoke-designed cabin hidden in a quiet Polish pine forest, less than an hour's drive from Warsaw.

To ensure complete surrender to the printed page, owners Bartłomiej Kraciuk and Marta Puchalska-Kraciuk lined the cabin's walls with bookcases filled with hundreds of books and put a yellow box in a prominent position in which to plonk their phones on arrival. It also helps that Wi-Fi reception is patchy and there's no television.

"When we bought the land and initially considered the design of the getaway, the first idea that came to mind was a cabin with a large window," says Bartłomiej, "but how long can you sit and stare out of a window? All day, if you are reading a book! Book reading is also a very special activity that relaxes the brain and helps one detach from the everyday hustle, even if it is a quick twenty-four-hour digital detox."

The nearly 5-metre-high (16.4-foot-high) window forms the front wall of the dwelling, allowing natural light to permeate the blonde timber-lined interiors. This promotes reading and quiet contemplation as well as offering a superb all-day view of grassy fields framed by leafy pines. Large shutters are easily moved into position to secure the cabin and provide privacy at night.

"We love the forests surrounding the house and did our best to preserve the natural environment as much as possible—the trees, the moss, the mulch. It gives a sense of being in the wild."

—Bartłomiej

"Book reading is a very special activity that relaxes the brain and helps one detach from the everyday hustle, even if it is a quick twenty-four-hour digital detox."

—*Bartłomiej*

Architect Marta and hospitality entrepreneur husband Bartłomiej adapted an original design by Pole Architekci, building the cabin as a rural escape, with the intention of finding peace and quiet away from their exceptionally busy lives in the city. They longed to unplug from the distractions of the internet so as to immerse themselves in nature, and to create the ideal conditions for reading, meditation, and to foster inspiration.

"On a daily basis we are super-busy people, engaged both in professional and family life," says Bartłomiej. "The days and weekends at the cabin are about not doing anything specific. It is a delightful moment to not have a plan or obligations, so we savour it. We also make it available for others to enjoy." (See page 284 for details.)

The snug 37-square-metre (398-square-foot) getaway over two levels cleverly incorporates an open sleeping loft above a well-planned living space with kitchenette. Access to the mezzanine bedroom is via a stained-timber staircase that smartly provides enough space underneath for a full bathroom. A cast-iron wood-burning heater keeps the cosy interior warm during the Polish winter. Sourcing local timbers for construction, the deck and roof are made from spruce, and the exteriors are clad in pine that has weathered to ash-grey, allowing the cabin to blend into its magical woodland setting.

"We love the forests surrounding the house," says Bartłomiej, "and did our best to preserve the natural environment as much as possible—the trees, the moss, the mulch. It gives a sense of being in the wild. Plus, there are little treats like mushroom picking without having to leave the terrace, and roe deer regularly pass right in front of the house."

Although the Bookworm Cabin was completed a couple of years ago as a couple's love nest and bibliophile's dream, Bartłomiej and Marta still visit with their two children (they have since built a larger cabin and are on to a new project as well).

"Our two young kids love the cabin even though the interior was not designed with them in mind," says Bartłomiej. "The hot wood-burning stove or stairs with no handrail look beautiful but require a conscious approach. The idea was to create a space for one or two people to calm all the senses, but it turns out the kids have that need, too! They love to spend time outside, carefully examining sticks and pine cones. We have lots of fun there."

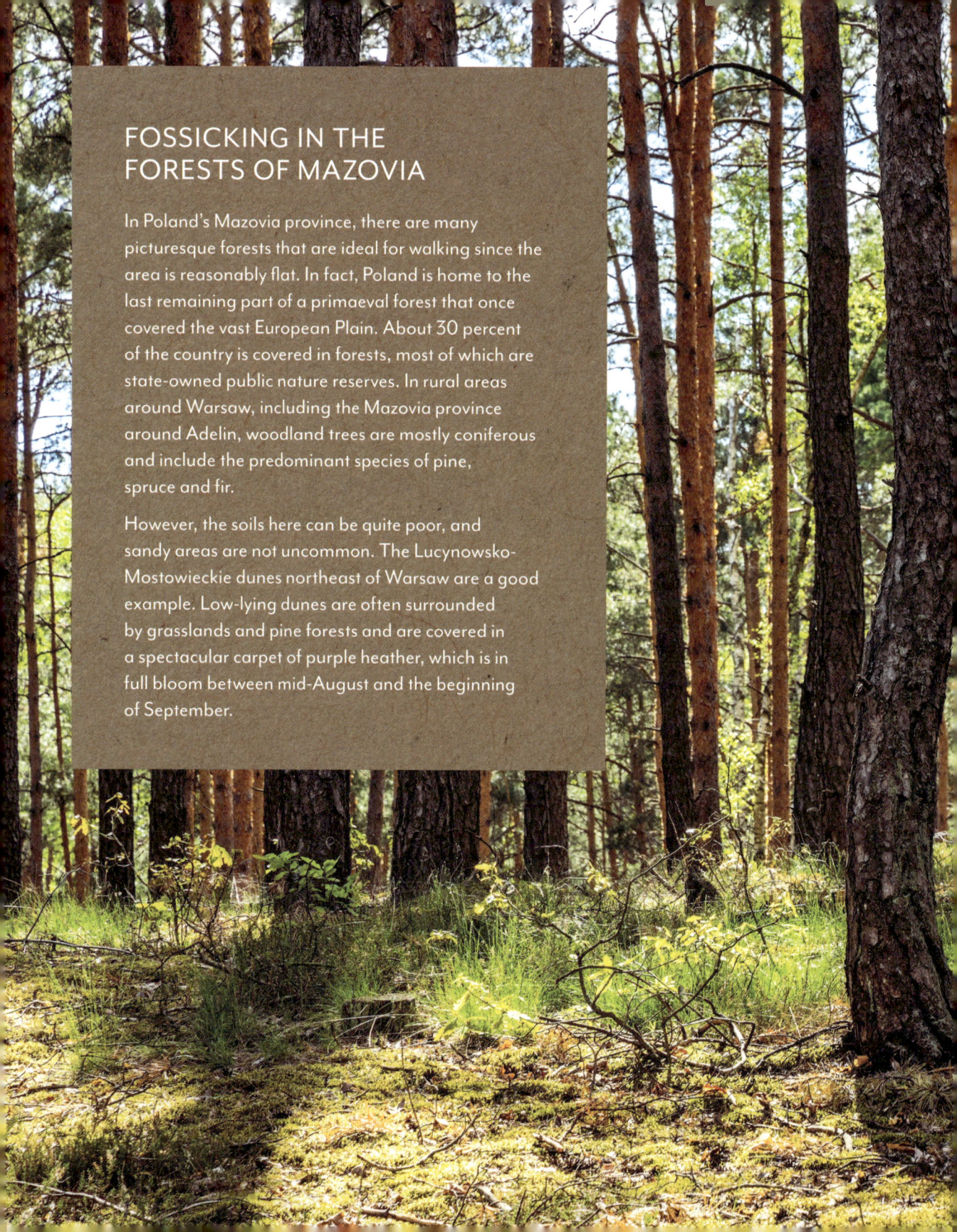

FOSSICKING IN THE FORESTS OF MAZOVIA

In Poland's Mazovia province, there are many picturesque forests that are ideal for walking since the area is reasonably flat. In fact, Poland is home to the last remaining part of a primaeval forest that once covered the vast European Plain. About 30 percent of the country is covered in forests, most of which are state-owned public nature reserves. In rural areas around Warsaw, including the Mazovia province around Adelin, woodland trees are mostly coniferous and include the predominant species of pine, spruce and fir.

However, the soils here can be quite poor, and sandy areas are not uncommon. The Lucynowsko-Mostowieckie dunes northeast of Warsaw are a good example. Low-lying dunes are often surrounded by grasslands and pine forests and are covered in a spectacular carpet of purple heather, which is in full bloom between mid-August and the beginning of September.

VINTERSPARV COTTAGE

Tisselskog, Dalsland, Sweden

The Swedish word *sagolikt* (meaning 'like a fairy tale') is how Linnea Klingström describes the traditional Swedish *röd stuga* (red country cottage) that she shares with lawyer husband Gustav Klingström and their two children, daughter Ingrid and son Arvid. *Vintersparv* ('winter sparrows' in English), as their country house is called, is the family's rural escape from city life in central Gothenburg.

Surrounded by the woodlands and farmlands of Dalsland, in the parish of Tisselskog (meaning 'whispering forest'), the little red cottage and its immediate environs wouldn't be out of place as a location in a Scandinavian fairy tale. For it's easy to imagine fairies and elves inhabiting the forest, water nymphs swimming in the nearby lake, *tomte* (gnomes and trolls) hiding in old barns.

Vintersparv serves as a writer's retreat for Linnea, an ethnologist, inspiring her work on a book about old Swedish ghost stories, and stirring her passion for Swedish legend, folklore and tradition. "I don't get any inspiration when we are in the city," she says. "When in Dalsland, the words come to me."

Surrounded by meadows and flowery fields, the cottage is located on an estate of roughly 4,500 square metres (1.2 acres), overlooking the serene waters of Råvarpen lake. "The lake is surrounded by forested mountains, giving rise to the most magical echoes," says Linnea. "Ingrid and Arvid love to go down to the lake, which they call their own. They take evening baths there in the summer to the sound of water birds."

As often as possible, the family (plus their two cats) drives two-and-a-half hours to spend weekends and holidays at the property. "There are no cars here, so the kids can run around without us parents being afraid," says Linnea.

As a writer and collector of Swedish folkloric artefacts, Linnea has stocked Vintersparv with Swedish books and historical objets d'art as much as for creative inspiration as for ready reference. Moody shadows and playful light beams flicker across the rooms, reminiscent of some of the homes featured in the existential and soul-searching films of Swedish director Ingmar Bergman.

In refurbishing the house's interiors, Linnea and Gustav decided to be true to the origins of the house, too, which was built around 1860, opting for simplicity, or as Linnea says, "a vintage look". This has been expressed in the use of muted dusty colours, traditional wallpapers and honest wooden furniture. "If the earlier habitants wanted to visit, they should recognise their house, albeit with a minor change in colours and so forth," she says.

Outside, the garden is dotted with apple and cherry trees. Linnea and Gustav have planted a vegetable garden, too. "We love to work in the garden," says Linnea. "We planned it for our noses as much as for our eyes. It smells of thyme, lemon balm, strawberry, rose, honeysuckle and elderflower. We regularly walk through the forest looking for wild mushrooms, plucking and eating wild strawberries. When we cook, we try to use what we have gathered outside, from herbs, salad greens and mushrooms to apples and berries."

"The best spot on our property
is the room of nature, where the sky is
our roof and the grass is our carpet."

—*Linnea*

During the day, the family stay outside as much as possible, enjoying the sunshine, physical activity and the visual delights each season brings.

"The seasons are so distinct," says Linnea. "During winter, all is embedded in deep snow, everything sparkles, and the nights are full of starlight and moonshine. In the mornings, the children like to follow the snowy tracks left by foxes, birds and mice. Sometimes a hare or a roe deer comes to visit. When the lake is covered by ice, it sounds as if it is singing or talking to us as it shifts—it makes weird, enchanting noises that are mesmerising."

In spring, the cranes arrive. The snow melts away and streams appear through the landscape, while the water in the lake rises. "Everything comes to life and the landscape turns from white to grey to green," says Linnea. "The farmers let out the cows and sheep to graze on open meadows, much to the children's enjoyment. In late spring, flowers bloom everywhere, and white and blue anemorte blanket the ground."

For Linnea, summer is the most beautiful season: "By day, the lake's water is warm and everything smells amazing. In the evening, the sky turns pink, and nights seem to last forever, filled with stars and moonshine. We pick elderflowers to make lemonade and cherries to make cherry jam. During summer, there are fruit and vegetables to pick, and the property provides endless toys for the kids, for example, trees make excellent climbing frames.

"Then comes autumn and the landscape takes on a mysterious intensity," says Linnea. "In the morning, the mist hangs heavy over the fields, reminding me of folk tales of elusive elves from Swedish mythology."

"Nothing is staged at Vintersparv," says Linnea. "It is as naturally beautiful as these pictures show. Our cottage is our paradise. We can hardly believe it is ours."

"Nothing is staged at Vintersparv, and the seasons are so distinct. It is as naturally beautiful as these pictures show."

—*Linnea*

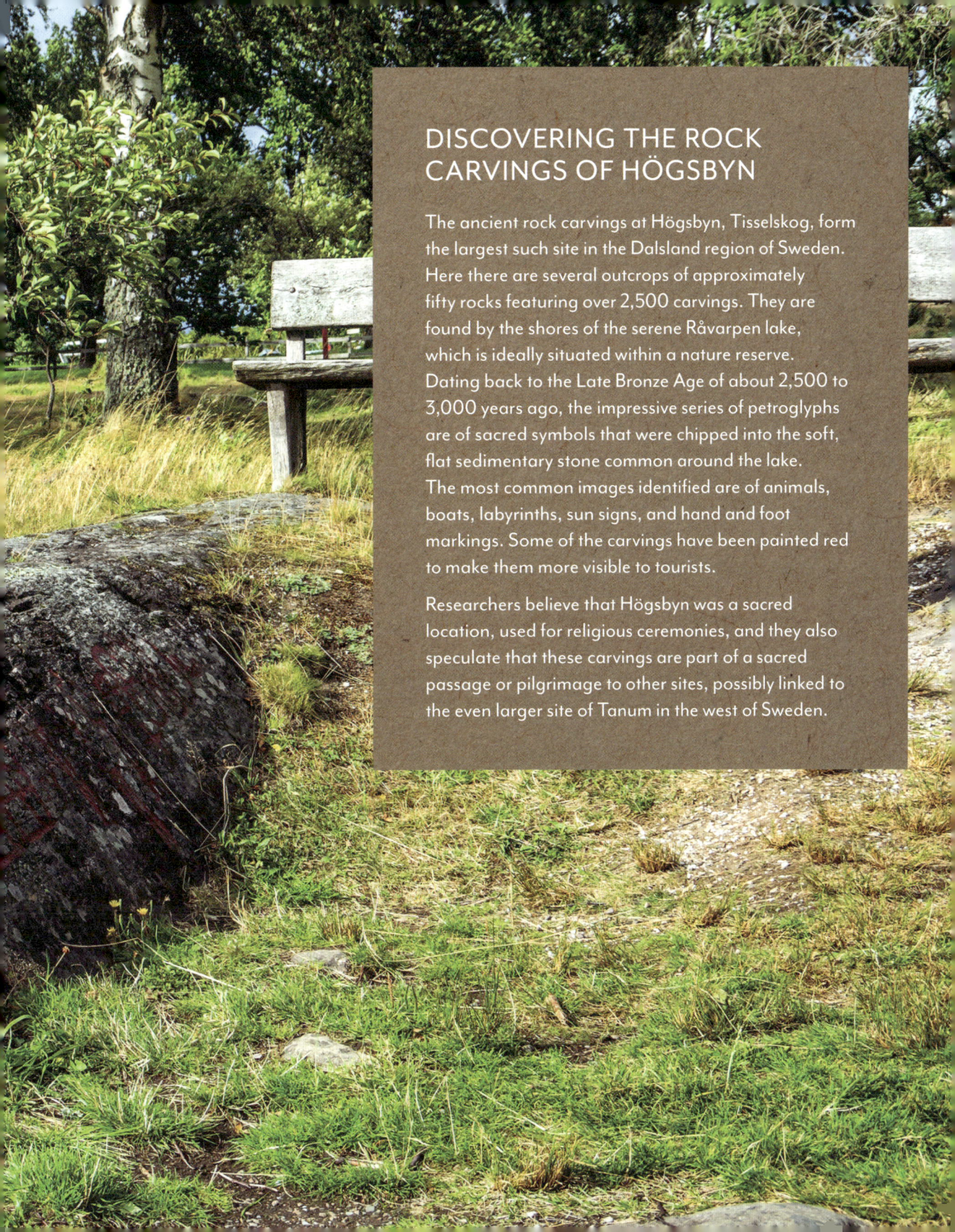

DISCOVERING THE ROCK CARVINGS OF HÖGSBYN

The ancient rock carvings at Högsbyn, Tisselskog, form the largest such site in the Dalsland region of Sweden. Here there are several outcrops of approximately fifty rocks featuring over 2,500 carvings. They are found by the shores of the serene Råvarpen lake, which is ideally situated within a nature reserve. Dating back to the Late Bronze Age of about 2,500 to 3,000 years ago, the impressive series of petroglyphs are of sacred symbols that were chipped into the soft, flat sedimentary stone common around the lake. The most common images identified are of animals, boats, labyrinths, sun signs, and hand and foot markings. Some of the carvings have been painted red to make them more visible to tourists.

Researchers believe that Högsbyn was a sacred location, used for religious ceremonies, and they also speculate that these carvings are part of a sacred passage or pilgrimage to other sites, possibly linked to the even larger site of Tanum in the west of Sweden.

THE NENE NEST

Kekaha Beach, Kauai, Hawaii, United States

It took decades of catching long flights back and forth across the Pacific Ocean to stay with family living on Kauai, Hawaii, for Seattle-based couple Melissa and Kyle Lipe to have it finally dawn on them to look for a getaway home on the island for themselves.

"We'd actually been looking for a vacation home closer to the Seattle area. Then one day, before a family trip, I flipped my search to Kauai out of curiosity. We got in touch with a local real estate agent (now one of our neighbours) who showed us the house that would become the Nene Nest."

In early 2020, the couple bought an original sugar plantation cottage on the sunny side of Kauai in Kekaha, and just thirty minutes away from family. It offered old-world Hawaiian charm for their family of four, with plenty of space for the energetic Madelyn (nine) and Henry (six) to play outside in the home's tropical gardens.

The family spruced up the cottage late in 2020, painting it and making minor repairs. Inside, they cleaned the original tiling and the polished wood floors; and decorated the white bright rooms with retro cane furniture and tropical prints. In the garden, overgrowth and weeds were removed, exposing tall red ginger plants, a hibiscus hedge walkway, a huge pink plumeria tree and several (edible) banana trees in the back.

Since then, the family have made many trips back to the island (each time mixing DIY housework with plenty of island playtime). "Now we just spend a lot of time as a family at the Nest, enjoying the slower pace of life on the island. My parents—the kids call them *tutu* ('grandparent' in Hawaiian)—come and go, and occasionally our entire island-based family arrives for a special get-together," says Melissa.

The Lipe family also like to share the 'Nest'. I hosted my mother's group getaway at the cottage and it was awesome," says Melissa. "Kyle's extended family members have vacationed there, too, as well as coworkers and friends. We also rent the cottage out to visitors to the island." (See details on page 285.)

"We take our mornings pretty slow at the Nest," says Melissa. "We make coffee and eat breakfast on the *lanai* (verandah) as a family. That usually includes some fresh fruit like papaya or pineapple from my dad's farm, tangerines from our neighbour, or bananas from our backyard patch. As the kids slowly get ready for a day out, I'll do a small project or two around the house while Kyle catches up on work. Most often, we throw on swimsuits, pack a lunch and spend the day at a secluded beach.

"We take our mornings pretty slow at the Nest. Often, we make coffee and breakfast and eat it on the *lanai* (verandah) as a family. That usually includes some fresh fruit like papaya or pineapple from my dad's farm."

—*Melissa*

"When we get home, we rinse in the outdoor shower, maybe take a nap or read in the garden lounge chairs and get ready for dinner. We always make sure to have Kalua pig and cabbage over rice at least once on our trip. It's a delicious local meal and even better if the *tutus* come over to enjoy it with us!"

It's a much slower, much more relaxed day than the family usually have at home in Seattle. "While at home we spend much of our time indoors," says Melissa. "We love to feel connected to the island here. As soon as you step off the plane in Kauai, you are embraced by warm breezes and wrapped in an intoxicating floral scent."

In Kauai, the Lipes often finish their day across the street at the ocean. "We keep our eye on what time sunset is and the kids will remind us when it's time to go," says Melissa. "We pour cocktails in to-go cups and walk across the street to take in the stunning sunsets that the west side offers."

BEACHCOMBING ON THE WEST COAST OF KAUAI

With 97 percent of Kauai covered by tropical forests or mountain ranges, it's not surprising this wild volcanic island also boasts some of Hawaii's most dramatic scenery, especially along the west coast. Particularly striking are the 1,220-metre-high (4,000-foot-high) Na Pali cliffs, which eventually culminate towards the more accessible southern end, in some of the longest stretches of yellow-sand beaches in Hawaii. The beach in the Polihale State Park, which can only be reached via a long dusty drive on an unpaved road, is uninhabited and surrounded by rugged headlands.

This marks the beginning of a 24-kilometre-long (15-mile-long) strip of beach that follows the coastline all the way to Kekaha, one of the small historic sugar plantation settlements in the southwest. Except in the sheltered parts, Kekaha Beach is more popular with fishermen and surfers than with swimmers due to an exposure to strong ocean swells and currents, but being relatively wide and uncrowded, it is a perfect location to go beachcombing, and, due to its west-facing position, the sunsets are spectacular.

HEMLOCK HOLLOW A-FRAME

Pocono Mountains, Pennsylvania, United States

The A-frame is an iconic American holiday home, which became the classic representation of leisure in the 1960s. So when New Yorkers Lauren Spear and Michael Goesele purchased a dilapidated one in the Pocono Mountains of northeastern Pennsylvania, the couple were determined to restore it with integrity.

"Being true to the vernacular of the building was really important to us," says Lauren. "Michael and I wanted to make sure the interiors harkened back to that time in subtle but updated ways; whether it's the midcentury furnishings, terrazzo tiles, or vintage art."

"We also thought it was critical to leave as much of the original wood showing as was possible, to let the house still tell its story," Michael adds.

"At first, we spent the weekdays in New York City for work and escaped 145 kilometres (90 miles) north to the mountain cabin on the weekends—but recently COVID-19 has flipped that ratio on its head, so we have spent a lot of time upstate," says Lauren. This meant the two could restore the A-frame while 'working from home'.

Hemlock Hollow is ever so softly nestled in a small clearing within two acres of mature towering trees—a dense canopy full of hemlock, oak, pine, and hickory—and dotted with craggy boulders, terrain typical of the Poconos.

The couple are both creatives. Lauren is an architectural designer, and Michael is a creative director. For these two, applying a little creative vision to 'rehab' a daggy old A-frame, while not without challenge, was right up their alley.

"The restoration and update of Hemlock Hollow has been an amazing chance for us to bring our creative worlds and skills together in a really meaningful and rewarding way," says Michael.

The small 12-metre x 8-metre (40-foot x 26-foot) structure was originally just a midcentury off-the-grid hunting cabin with no water or electricity. It took months of removing layer after layer of makeshift construction, walls, ceilings, and materials, in order to just get down to the basic A-shaped envelope.

"There's something so honest about the A-frame structure: what you see is what you get," continues Lauren. "Standing in the ribcage of floor-to-ceiling beams that run down the length of the space, we knew our job was to let in all the natural light we could. With six skylights, two windows, and four 3.7-metre x 1.8-metre (12-foot x 6-foot) custom-made panels of glass later, we feel like the structure can now breathe."

Michael and Lauren both have a pretty eclectic sense of style. Lauren has a great appreciation for design history and architecture, and Michael has a deep love for art and graphic design. "We feel like this juxtaposition of vintage and contemporary worked well in the A-frame," says Michael. "From every book on the shelves, to every piece of art on the wall—there is a story of us that we love to celebrate whenever we spend downtime here."

Typically, Lauren and Michael start their day lazily sitting on the Hemlock Hollow porch, drinking coffee, eating lots of pancakes, and often returning to the cocoon of the loft for a catnap before noon. Afternoons are spent adventuring, hiking with their Vizsla pup, Bernie, enjoying the surrounding trails, rivers and waterfalls of the Poconos, or venturing into a nearby town to enjoy the burgeoning cultural scene. During the evenings the couple love to cook, do puzzles, play old records, then conclude by getting cosy around a fire in the woodstove or outdoor firepit.

"The outdoor firepit is 100 percent our favourite spot," says Lauren. "We always say 'fires are the best form of therapy'. Whether that's under the stars, sun, snow, or string lights, sitting near a fire at night is such a ritualistic way to decompress, celebrate, and share. There's something about the crackling glow that is so satisfyingly multisensory and all-consuming—everything else fades away."

In Hemlock Hollow, Lauren and Michael have found their perfect escape: "This home is so intimate and small. It was intended as a nest for the two of us, as a place of refuge, so we could disconnect from the world and reconnect with each other."

"This home is so intimate and small. It was intended as a nest for the two of us, as a place of refuge, so we could disconnect from the world and reconnect with each other."

—Lauren

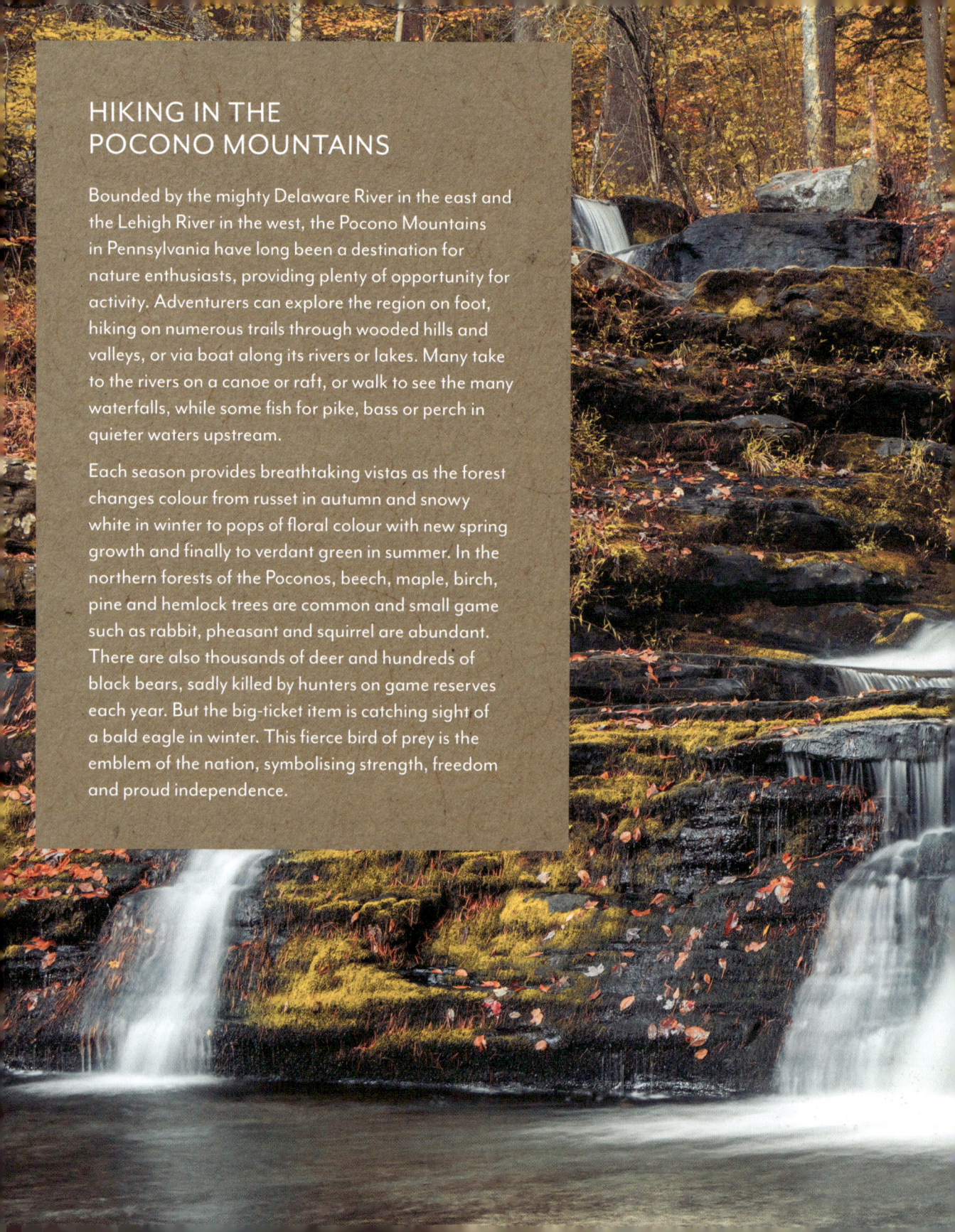

HIKING IN THE POCONO MOUNTAINS

Bounded by the mighty Delaware River in the east and the Lehigh River in the west, the Pocono Mountains in Pennsylvania have long been a destination for nature enthusiasts, providing plenty of opportunity for activity. Adventurers can explore the region on foot, hiking on numerous trails through wooded hills and valleys, or via boat along its rivers or lakes. Many take to the rivers on a canoe or raft, or walk to see the many waterfalls, while some fish for pike, bass or perch in quieter waters upstream.

Each season provides breathtaking vistas as the forest changes colour from russet in autumn and snowy white in winter to pops of floral colour with new spring growth and finally to verdant green in summer. In the northern forests of the Poconos, beech, maple, birch, pine and hemlock trees are common and small game such as rabbit, pheasant and squirrel are abundant. There are also thousands of deer and hundreds of black bears, sadly killed by hunters on game reserves each year. But the big-ticket item is catching sight of a bald eagle in winter. This fierce bird of prey is the emblem of the nation, symbolising strength, freedom and proud independence.

THE MODERNS

Displaying remarkable architectural design inspired by stunning locations, these modern romantic getaways for couples and their families promise a slow-living experience—with views to die for! Incorporating sleek interiors and decorated with cherished artworks, these minimalist abodes not only offer owners a respite from urban living, but an opportunity to connect with family in a serene, unhurried setting. Sustainable construction features, local materials and off-grid elements honour the environment, while expansive windows characteristically frame panoramic views of snowy mountains, desert boulder formations, expansive surf beaches, tropical groves, dense jungles or cloud forests.

BAKER BOYS BEACH HOUSE

North Stradbroke Island, Queensland, Australia

If ever there was a place to explore the quality of permanent camping in architectural form, it is on North Stradbroke Island, also known by its Aboriginal name of Minjerribah. Hundreds of campsites overlook kilometres of white sandy beaches. And, due to the island being just 40 kilometres (25 miles) and a short ferry ride away from Queensland's capital of Brisbane, it is dotted with simple 'weekenders' or holiday houses built as boltholes for the nine-to-five crowd escaping the city.

"Since the Baker Boys Beach House was co-commissioned by three families to share, the influence of local campsites, where cooking, gathering and sleeping zones are united under the one tarp, informed both the layout and the exterior design," says Erhard Rathmayr, the project's lead architect and creative director of Refresh Design. "We also intended it to be reminiscent of the beach shack vernacular, a typical style of house built on Stradbroke Island from the 1960s to the '90s."

Suggestive of a bush camp tent, a black steel butterfly roof hovers above the deliberately simple box structure allowing light to permeate living spaces from high windows tucked just beneath it. Charred timber cladding was chosen to reflect the home's environment, while also addressing bushfire requirements.

A simple floor plan accommodates each family group on their respective visits by dividing the house east to west by a hallway, which separates four bedrooms and two bathrooms on one side from the large open living space on the other.

Turning the Baker Boys Beach House design into reality was a collaborative effort: a member of each family co-owns Bespoke Constructions, the company that coordinated the build, while Vicki Dubois of Flokk Interiors, and wife to Frederic Dubois of Bespoke, designed the interiors (see page 285 for details).

For Vicki it was important the interior fabrication would stand up to wear and tear. "It needed to be hard-wearing and practical, which is why we chose robust materials that don't need much cleaning."

"The shower stalls are open, no glass, and the kitchen cabinets are laminated, because it's long-lasting," says Vicki. "We chose hardwood floors internally and concrete for the patio out back. Decoratively, the rooms are deliberately minimalist."

Located on a very steep slope, the back of the house is anchored to the ground, where it is well connected to the adjoining bushland reserve, most often enjoyed from a sheltered sitting area featuring a firepit. The other end of the structure is cantilevered to take full advantage of sweeping ocean views, while providing covered space for car parking and storage facilities underneath.

"There's an incredible view from the open-plan living space," says Vicki. "We look over treetops, with no development in front of us, straight out to the ocean and horizon. It's such a rarefied kind of experience; just breathtaking."

Since the footprint of the two-level house is compact, and there can be up to ten people there at any one time, the communal spaces in the house are utilitarian: "They are for cooking, sleeping, showering and talking, just like when you go camping with families."

"That sense of being together is a really important factor for us on holiday. Fred and I were looking for a place where we could build family memories for our eleven-year-old son, Oliver." Belgium-born Frederic recalls family trips through Europe, skylarking with his two brothers, and Vicki remembers beach holidays on the coast of New South Wales, Australia, with her sister.

BAKER BOYS BEACH HOUSE

Now on most trips to the island the couple are joined by sister Kelly, her husband Bill, and their two kids. "We spend the day at the beach and all end up eating and having drinks on the deck. It's fantastic to see Ollie sharing those moments with cousins and friends," says Frederic.

"Lumped in together can get a bit messy, but that's the whole purpose of going to the island, isn't it? To live communally, to unplug," adds Vicki. "We don't have Wi-Fi, there's no television, and apart from an occasional downloaded movie we watch together, the kids are rarely allowed devices."

"This is where creativity is born," says Vicki. The kids will often put on impromptu plays at the back of the house with the bush as their backdrop, or guitars will be played while others sit on the curved step, gathered around the firepit.

From the deck of the house, Frederic likes to survey the swells of Cylinder Beach, deciding on whether he takes his board down the 800-metre (2,625-foot) steep incline or drives over to Main Beach to surf. At other times, he'll go fishing with a mate, or take the kids and dog on a hike though the bush, or to the beach, where they might stop momentarily to find 'pippies' (shellfish), found by twisting feet into the soft shoreline sand. "The rhythm of our days is really slow," he says.

Vicki prefers to visit the gentler sandy coves for swimming. She loves to walk with kids and friends along the headland trail to capture the most dramatic views of the ocean and natural bush landscape on her camera. As the bush hides some venomous snakes and spiders, it's important for the children to learn to be mindful and respectful of their environment, but then again there are friendly creatures, too.

"Sometimes, I get up for my morning run," says Frederic, "and the kangaroos, occasionally with babies in the pouch, are feeding on grass, right outside our door. It's pretty special."

"Koalas in the gum trees and kangaroos hopping through the bush and beach—what's not to love?" says Vicki.

"We look over treetops, with no development in front of us, straight out to the ocean and horizon. It's such a rarefied kind of experience; just breathtaking."

—*Vicki*

MEETING THE WILDLIFE
OF STRADBROKE ISLAND

North Stradbroke Island is a wildlife wonderland. The natural bushland that blankets the island is home to some of Australia's most beloved animals, including kangaroos, koalas, wallabies, bandicoots and echidnas. There are also turtles and lizards, several frog species and hundreds of birds. Dolphins are numerous and there are plenty of whales to spot during their migratory seasons mid-year.

The traditional owners of North Stradbroke Island, the Quandamooka people, have taken a lead role in the conservation of the flora and fauna of the island, which is increasingly known by its Aboriginal name of Minjerribah. Now 1,400 hectares (3,459 acres) of bushland on Minjerribah is under Aboriginal title and registered in the Land for Wildlife program.

This means that the more than 450 species of native animals on the island have a protected refuge. As the only naturally occurring island koalas in Australia, the genetically distinct koala population on Minjerribah has benefitted from these initiatives by being kept largely disease-free. Like other native animals on the island, such as the kangaroos and wallabies, these marsupials were isolated on the island about 8,000 years ago after the last sea-level rise.

HALFMOON BAY CABIN

British Columbia, Canada

The wedding celebrations for Patrick Warren and Kevin Kaufman couldn't have been held in a more romantic setting. With a majestic view of Halfmoon Bay in British Columbia, Canada, before them, and with a sleek modern cabin serving as their backdrop, the wedding party and guests sat around sumptuously decorated tables toasting the newlyweds. As the proceedings continued, the couple's black Douglas fir–clad cabin, was dramatically sidelit by the warm yellow rays of a waning sun, the blonde wood interiors glowed and the towering trees encircling this idyllic scene swayed gently in a warm summer breeze.

Surrounded by cedar trees, the cabin, which architect Patrick had designed for the pair, rests on a one-acre waterfront property, just a forty-minute ferry ride across the stunning Strait of Georgia from the couple's home base of Vancouver. Patrick, a partner of the architectural firm Frits de Vries Architects + Associates (see page 285 for details), and Kevin, a scientist, translated their love of design with their desire to commune with nature by creating the stress-free getaway in order to temporarily escape urban living.

"The house is designed as a holiday home for us, and our English Labrador, Taavi (which means 'beloved'), a sort of spiritual retreat in nature," says Patrick.

Despite its proximity to the city, the cabin feels remote, and yet there is a small friendly community nearby. It's the kind of place where organic produce is sold from roadside stands and seafood is purchased from local fishermen. "Kevin likes to cook what we buy; whatever is in season," says Patrick.

The couple's activities include hiking on misty winter days and in autumn, gardening and watching the plants emerge in springtime, and exploring the beaches and kayaking in summer. "In a rural environment, there is a stronger connection to nature, so every activity we do here is influenced by weather and season," says Patrick. "We are very aware of the length of the days and the quality of moonlight on a clear night. In the summer, we spend more time at the cabin, working remotely, and even though summer is relatively short, it's impossibly beautiful. Half of our waterfront is a small beach cove, where we were married, and the other half is a granite shelf, perfect for sunbathing. It is difficult to return to the city."

Spotting wildlife is one of Patrick and Kevin's favourite pastimes at Halfmoon Bay cabin: "We have families of deer browsing the property. Eagles, ravens and bats frequent the trees. River otters swim in the ocean with us. We also see seals, sea lions, orcas, humpbacks and grey whales."

A short kayak across the water from the beach is Merry Island. "We love to paddle around the lighthouse on the island and see the amazing number of sea birds and seals on the other side", says Patrick. Likewise, ancient mossy forests are a short hike in any direction from the cabin's front door. Sometimes, the wildlife gets a little too friendly for Patrick and Kevin. "One day we received photo notification from our smart doorbell that 'a person' was at the door. However, it was a large black bear lumbering down our front steps!" exclaims Patrick.

The expansive glass windows of the cabin allow the couple to feel like they are outside all year, watching storms, spotting whales and checking for bears. The cabin faces south to capture light but its layout is multidirectional, meaning the structure provides views of the ocean and the lighthouse of Merry Island out front while also looking back into the woodland behind and sideways into the garden.

The geometry of the house is arranged simply, with the public spaces being flanked on one side by the main bedroom suite and on the other side by the guest bedroom accommodation. There are often visitors. "We tend to only host two or three friends at a time, so the connection we share at the cabin and in the natural surroundings is intimate and meaningful for all of us, and takes them away from the pressures of urban life."

"This was to be a house for gathering with friends where we could cast off our social pressures and expectations. It would also be a place to escape into tranquillity and to see ourselves as a part of nature."

—Patrick

"The materials were chosen for their simplicity and tactility," says Patrick, "for their ability to connect our bodies to the space and bring us back to nature." For example, the exterior of the house is black, so that it disappears into the forest shadows (the house is invisible from the water). "The contrast of the black exterior with the light lye-washed cedar wall interiors provides the illusion that there is more light during dim coastal winters," he says.

The home's colour palette was inspired by the site: from the dark woods behind to the beach cove with its sun-and-sea-bleached driftwood and light-grey granite rock outcrops. The interior wood tones are complemented with furnishings and fittings of light terracotta (the colour of their native Arbutus tree), dusty pinks, soft whites, beiges and blacks, accented by vintage 1970s to '90s pieces, sourced by Kevin. Home accessories include baskets in sea-grass, blankets in naturally dyed wool and local and Japanese handmade stoneware ceramics.

The artwork in the home is exclusively from the region, and the closet doors and headboard are bespoke super-graphic lime-plaster panels. "We want to be surrounded by meaningful, beautiful objects that show the hand of the artist," says Patrick.

Although Patrick and Kevin love living in the city, enjoying the many social events, restaurants and amenities on offer, they know that being in nature is essential for them: "The cabin is a place of freedom to let our guards down with good friends, and to allow the wildness of nature to seep back into us."

"The artwork in the home is exclusively from the region, including a large charcoal rubbing displayed in the main bedroom and small bronze sculptures found in the bedroom and living room, which are by my great aunt, Elza Mayhew, an accomplished midcentury Canadian artist."

—*Patrick*

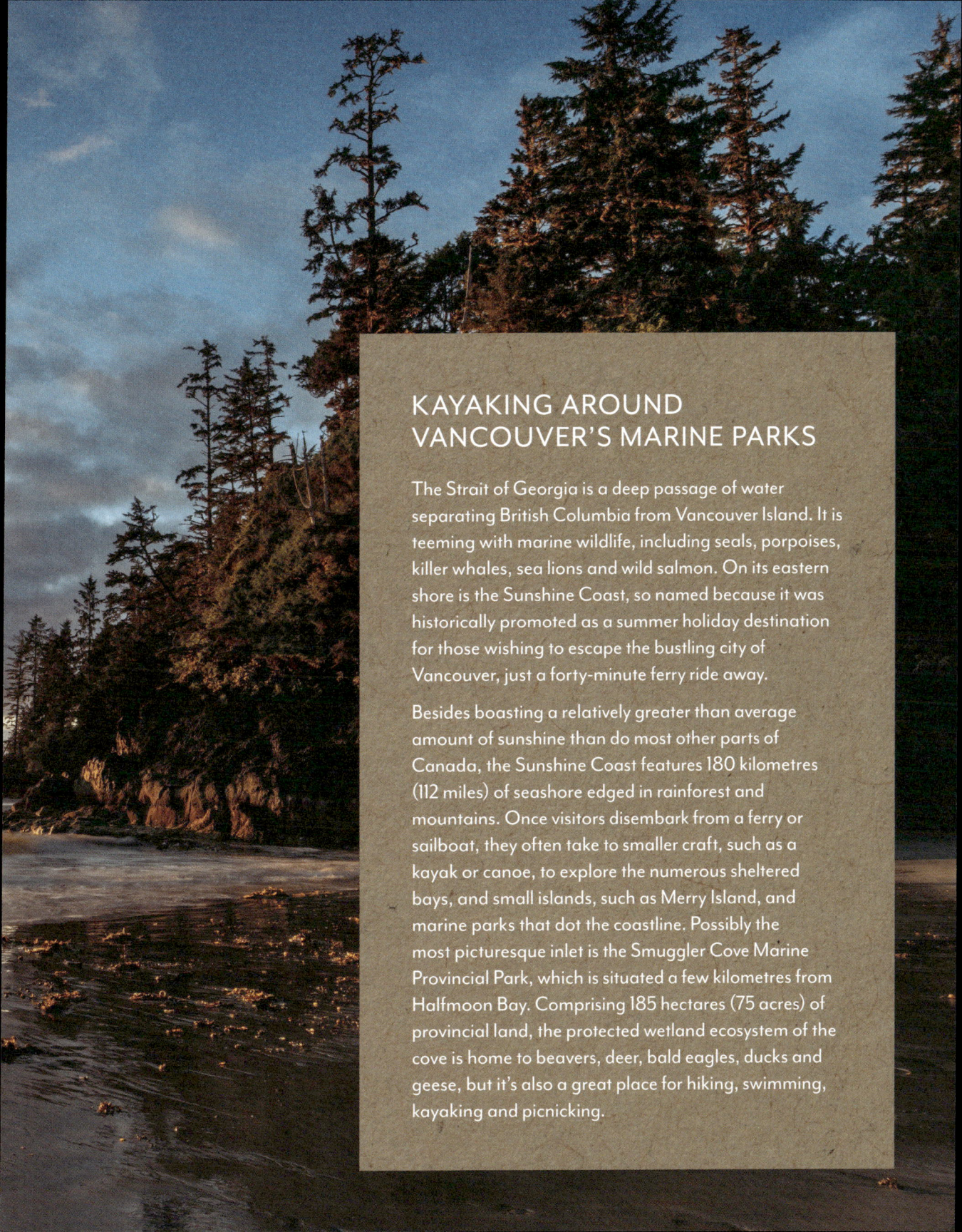

KAYAKING AROUND VANCOUVER'S MARINE PARKS

The Strait of Georgia is a deep passage of water separating British Columbia from Vancouver Island. It is teeming with marine wildlife, including seals, porpoises, killer whales, sea lions and wild salmon. On its eastern shore is the Sunshine Coast, so named because it was historically promoted as a summer holiday destination for those wishing to escape the bustling city of Vancouver, just a forty-minute ferry ride away.

Besides boasting a relatively greater than average amount of sunshine than do most other parts of Canada, the Sunshine Coast features 180 kilometres (112 miles) of seashore edged in rainforest and mountains. Once visitors disembark from a ferry or sailboat, they often take to smaller craft, such as a kayak or canoe, to explore the numerous sheltered bays, and small islands, such as Merry Island, and marine parks that dot the coastline. Possibly the most picturesque inlet is the Smuggler Cove Marine Provincial Park, which is situated a few kilometres from Halfmoon Bay. Comprising 185 hectares (75 acres) of provincial land, the protected wetland ecosystem of the cove is home to beavers, deer, bald eagles, ducks and geese, but it's also a great place for hiking, swimming, kayaking and picnicking.

CASA SALVAJE

Palmichal de Acosta, Costa Rica

Nestled in the mountains of Palmichal de Acosta, and surrounded by cloud forest, lies Lilly Peña's retreat, Casa Salvaje. Also known as Wild House, this brutalist off-grid haven was designed by Lilly's close friend the architect María de la Paz Alice, founder of Mazpazz Arquitectura (see page 285 for details). Despite the logistical challenges that María's team encountered constructing the self-sustaining stone-and-concrete project in a remote location, the brief from Lilly was simple: she wanted an artistic haven in which to disconnect from city life in San José and commune with nature.

María's modernist design was completed in 2021. It is both pragmatic and honest, in terms of materials used, and spiritual, by way of creating a transcendental living experience for Lilly, a Costa Rican film producer. María also ensured she framed Lilly's beloved rainforest views via a series of geometrical portals, the most striking of which is located in the concrete entrance courtyard, which is known as the 'vortex'. Here, two large circular openings, one cut to reveal mountain views and the other opening up to the sky, create a dramatic focal point to the house, softened only by its use as a greenhouse for ferns, mountain orchids and other endemic species.

"The 'vortex' is one my favourite parts of the house," says Lilly. "The walls are made of raw brutalist concrete featuring leaf stamps we made using vegetation collected from the forest and crystals encrusted in the concrete floor! Here I feel the true energy of the mountains. I have a perfect view of the horizon, the sky at night with hundreds of stars, the clouds passing by overhead, and of course the thunderstorms!"

Given the house's secluded location, it was also vital María incorporated the use of local materials and craftsmanship. Local stone was used on some exterior walls, and the wood-shingled roof was handmade on-site with Costa Rican teak. The interiors of the two-bedroom house are covered entirely from floor to ceiling in a local wood called 'roble coral', which María likens to walking into a wooden womb.

Responding to Lilly's environmental concerns, and the practicality of the remote location having no power or water services, María ensured the house would be completely off-grid, relying on solar energy for power and on spring water captured uphill on the property. The landscaping by Jorge Salgado was designed as an edible and medicinal garden, with springwater pools and endemic species.

The interior design was the work of Lilly's friend interior designer Ileana Guerrero, whose use of handmade elements, local handicrafts and eclectic pieces is a reflection of Lilly's bohemian sensibility.

"I wanted a simple, cosy and ethnical space, filled with items I'd collected from Costa Rica and abroad," says Lilly. "Ileana very creatively curated my pieces and added more beautiful ones of her own design, all handmade by local artisans and weavers. Most of our furniture is made of local timbers by artisans in the area."

When Lilly is not in the 'vortex' or relaxing on the wide verandah in contemplation, and enjoying the stillness, she loves to invite others to join her meditation sessions, share her intimate dinners or to take part in the deep conversations that seem to effortlessly take place at Casa Salvaje.

"I enjoy the house with my family, including my three children Camille, Stephan and Natalia, and our gorgeous dogs—some of which I rescued from city streets. We love to hang out or go hiking in the mountains. My close friends come to visit often. We'll talk, eat and gaze at the stars by the firepit. María comes, too. She is a great friend and a truly amazing architect who has been wonderful to collaborate with. The two of us visited the site often to share ideas about creating the ideal escape. I trusted her vision."

Since Lilly also visits Casa Salvaje solo, her days on the mountain are committed to a slow-living lifestyle. "I usually start with music and a cup of tea, then walk around the garden to check the plants and look for birds, bees and butterflies. If I'm lucky, I can find a morpho (a big blue butterfly endemic to the mountain), I visit my neighbours, their orchards, then sit on the terrace to watch the sun set."

Nature-lover Lilly founded the organic farmers' market Mercado KM0 in an effort to promote the natural produce of the area, but she is best known in Costa Rica for her documentary film making, specifically dedicated to the protection of the oceans. It is in the cool mountainous central rainforests, however, where she has found her ultimate happy place: "I immediately fell in love with the peacefulness of this location. It was the perfect spot to build a hideaway where I could take my family, friends and dogs to enjoy the forest, the rivers, the purity of the air and the natural springwaters. I love the energy, the view of the mountain, the light at sunset, the moon shadow and stars. It's as romantic as it sounds. I could be worlds away."

"I fell in love with the peacefulness of this location immediately. It was the perfect place to build my hideaway where I could take my family, friends and dogs to enjoy the forest, the rivers, the purity of the air and the natural spring waters."

—*Lilly*

THE MODERNS   CASA SALVAJE   153

WALKING THROUGH THE CLOUD FORESTS OF COSTA RICA

Much of the tropical paradise of Costa Rica is covered by lush rainforests and shrouded in mysterious cloud forests. The rainforests typically hug the coast, have wide rivers and are teeming with exotic wildlife. In contrast, the cooler cloud forests are found at altitudes of 1,000 to 2,500 metres (3,280 to 8,200 feet). These rare, beautiful forests possess fast-running rivers and waterfalls and are often blanketed by a fine mist formed by the condensation that occurs when vapour created in the humid environment circulates between the deep valleys and steep mountains. While the Monteverde Cloud Forest Biological Reserve in northern Costa Rica is perhaps the world's most famous, there is cloud forest to explore within an hour out of the sprawling centrally located capital of San José.

With over half a million species of wildlife, most of which are insects, Costa Rica is one of the world's most biodiverse countries. For example, 10 percent of known butterfly species reside in Costa Rica, including the blue morpho. The rich diversity is hidden in the mist-veiled foliage of the central highland cloud forests, which is home to mammals such as jaguar and other wild cat species, sloths, deer, tapir, bats, monkeys, and birds, such as hummingbirds and quetzal.

CASITA JABIN

Valladolid, Yucatán, Mexico

Rising from the subtropical jungles of the Yucatán Peninsula is a stacked pair of pink cubes forming a contemporary one-bedroom getaway. Featuring a restrained design aesthetic, a private plunge pool and a cool interior, it's the perfect place for owners Anette Urbina Gamboa and husband Eduardo De la Peña Corral to rest, unplug and retreat from their busy corporate lives in Mexico City.

"I grew up in the Yucatán and Eduardo lived there for many years, so we both have a special love for this region," says Anette. "Our dream was to create a place to reconnect us to our roots, inspired by the places we have stayed in while travelling."

The couple commissioned the Mérida city-based architectural firm TACO (see page 286 for details) to design the house. TACO's objective was to achieve "a reflective and contemplative place that links the owners with the surrounding wild landscape."

In harmony with its natural surroundings, the house was built using traditional construction techniques utilising local materials. The footprint is only 42 square metres (452 square feet) but by erecting a double-height structure, the design could accommodate a mezzanine bedroom upstairs and a kitchen and living space downstairs, which opens to a furnished terrace and the pool. The whole structure was elevated on a platform, making it difficult for wildlife to access. Finally, the rough stucco exterior was painted a watermelon pink, a common colour choice for Mexican villas.

For Anette, it was important to incorporate a tasteful and curated interior design, highlighting Mexican design brands and local artisan handicrafts. "We felt the interior design should be simple and toned down, not only to let the architectural form speak for itself, but also to contrast with the dramatic pink hue of the exterior."

The house is located on a hectare of land filled with Jabin trees, a species typical of the Yucatán. "When deciding where to build the house, we placed it near a particularly beautiful Jabin tree, so it would shade the terrace and pool area," says Anette. "As the project took shape, the tree ended up becoming part of the soul of the house, which is why we named it Casita Jabin."

Close to the beautiful Spanish colonial town of Valladolid, near ancient Mayan pyramids and a walk away from the otherworldly waterhole Cenote Suytun, the house provides a holiday base for Anette and Eduardo to see old friends and visit some of the local towns and attractions; as well as a relaxing place to cherish family time together with baby daughter Isabella.

"We love to enjoy the house as a family, hanging out by the pool, listening to music and drinking very cold wine!" says Anette. "One of us can nap in the outdoors hammock while the other cooks dinner. But as we are often in the city, we love to share our space with guests from all around the world." (See page 286 for details.)

"Staying at the house allows us to disconnect, live life at a slower pace and marvel at life's small pleasures: a sunset, the wind, a pink sky, the sound of birds, a cooling swim on a hot day or the shining stars at night. Casita Jabin brings us peace."

"Our dream was to create a place to reconnect us to our Yucatán roots, inspired by the places we have stayed in while travelling."

—*Anette*

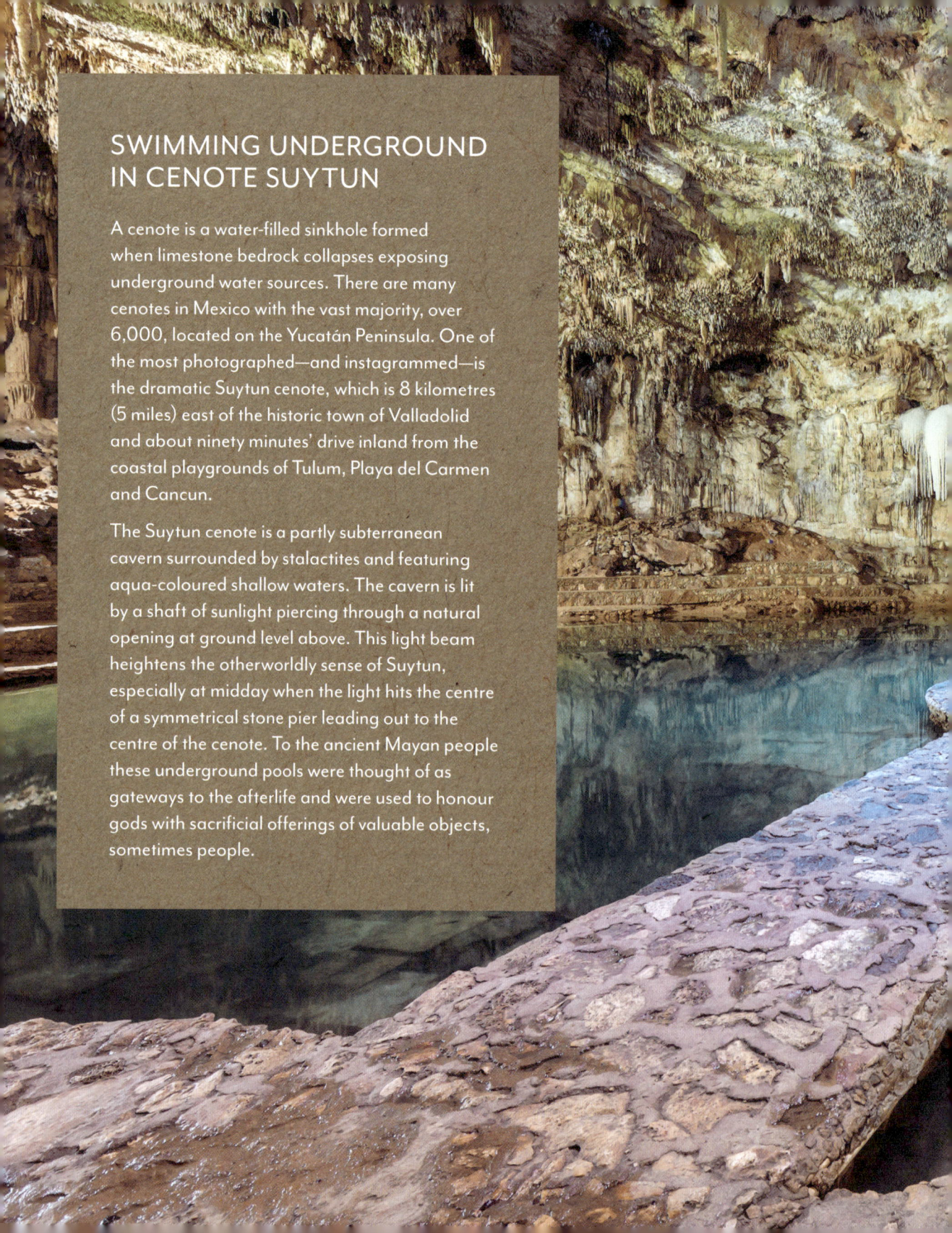

SWIMMING UNDERGROUND IN CENOTE SUYTUN

A cenote is a water-filled sinkhole formed when limestone bedrock collapses exposing underground water sources. There are many cenotes in Mexico with the vast majority, over 6,000, located on the Yucatán Peninsula. One of the most photographed—and instagrammed—is the dramatic Suytun cenote, which is 8 kilometres (5 miles) east of the historic town of Valladolid and about ninety minutes' drive inland from the coastal playgrounds of Tulum, Playa del Carmen and Cancun.

The Suytun cenote is a partly subterranean cavern surrounded by stalactites and featuring aqua-coloured shallow waters. The cavern is lit by a shaft of sunlight piercing through a natural opening at ground level above. This light beam heightens the otherworldly sense of Suytun, especially at midday when the light hits the centre of a symmetrical stone pier leading out to the centre of the cenote. To the ancient Mayan people these underground pools were thought of as gateways to the afterlife and were used to honour gods with sacrificial offerings of valuable objects, sometimes people.

KAWAU ISLAND BACH

Harris Bay, Kawau Island, Hauraki Gulf, New Zealand

Access to Kawau Island relies on a short sea voyage, which is why the small number of holiday homes there—known as bachs in New Zealand—are found dotted along the coastline. This guarantees bach owners a water view, and since most of the island is bush, a leafy green backdrop, as well. There's also a sense of being 'off the beaten track' even though the island is just 40 kilometres (25 miles) north of the bustling city of Auckland.

Attracted to the island's calm, crystal-clear waters, city-based seafarers often drop anchor in the many sheltered coves to go swimming and fishing. This is almost how professional couple Greg Knowles, an accountancy partner, and his wife Dr Alison Knowles first discovered the island thirty years ago when they found safe harbour in the island's tranquil Harris Bay after a rough sailing trip down the coast from the Bay of Islands. "Twenty years later we bought a lot here and camped for a couple of summers until we built our bach," says Greg.

Commissioning Crosson Architects (see page 286 for details) to design a sophisticated but 'pared back' hut to capitalise on the views, while being robust enough to comfortably accommodate their then three energetic teenage sons, Greg and Alison settled on building a design inspired by the humble boat shed. Shipping materials in from the mainland, a corrugated-iron-clad structure was eventually constructed that rested lightly on a raised wooden platform just metres from the shoreline. Greg describes it as "a small but highly functional dwelling retaining the brief's theme of refinement in a remote location."

The most striking feature of the bach is the large translucent corrugated polycarbonate panels on the façade. "Intentionally allowing an obscured view of the home pod within by day, the panels provide a lantern-like quality to the front deck at night, and extend the deck when open, to provide greater privacy to the interior and protection from the elements," says lead architect Sam Caradus of his award-winning design. "In addition to using a series of solid shutters and doors to conceal the interior, the translucent panels can slide shut and the entire house closed down to provide security when not occupied."

"Our island neighbours fly flags to let visiting friends know they are in residence," says Greg. "We simply open the double-height, steel-framed, bi-folding front doors. They are incredibly heavy but easy to operate. The engineering behind them is impressive."

In contrast to the cool corrugated exterior, the warm and cosy interior of the bach is lined in smooth hoop pine plywood and features solid oak flooring. There are 150 square metres (1,615 square feet) of living over two levels. On the ground floor, sliding door panels positioned either side of a central hallway connect or partition spaces, while large wooden decks out front and back provide additional dining spots. Upstairs, three bedrooms offer attractive views of the peaceful bay or dense bush. Décor is minimal.

"From the galvanised pipe and stainless-steel fittings to the plywood bedside tables, we kept interior design simple. There's no need for art on the walls when you have so much aquatic movement out front."

—*Greg*

"From the galvanised pipe and stainless-steel fittings to the plywood bedside tables, we followed Sam's advice and kept the interior design simple," says Greg. "There is no need for art on the walls when you have so much aquatic movement out front."

Now that the Knowles' sons are young adults, they periodically take over the Kawau bach. "It sleeps eight to ten people and the overflow set up camp in tents and sleeping bags on the front lawn or on the 'village green' at the end of the bay. It's a free-for-all!" laughs Greg.

When it's just Alison and Greg on-site, she likes to tinker in the garden, while Greg's favourite part of bach life is chopping firewood and lighting fires for the wood-fired cedar hot tub and the pizza oven out the back.

Greg says the couple also host friends and extended family, taking them "fishing, or kayaking around the island, or paddle boarding over to the Kawau Boating Club on the other side of the bay for a beer."

Walking is always on the agenda, with or without family. "We hike through the mānuka and pine forest up the back of our place to Mansion House Bay or the copper mine," says Greg. "We're delighted to see bird-life returning, especially endemic species. We have tūī, kererū and kākā buzzing around our place, and our neighbours have spotted the elusive kiwi in the bush up the back!"

BIRDWATCHING KIWIS ON KAWAU ISLAND

Named after the Māori word for the shag, Kawau Island is home to many bird species. Along the coastline, visiting sea birds, such as shags, cormorants, gannets, kingfishers, terns and gulls are often seen dive-bombing for fish, perching on warm rocks in the coves or patrolling the island's beaches. The Kawau shag nests in the glorious red-flowering coast-hugging pōhutukawa trees, and little blue penguins are occasionally spotted around the shoreline.

Native birds (and a few Australian interlopers, such as kookaburras and rosellas, which were introduced a century ago) can be found throughout the island's extensive bushland. Hike or tramp (as New Zealanders like to say) through the island's lush green interior and you might see or hear the cry or warble of the tūī, pīwakawaka, kererū, morepork, silver-eye, or grey warbler. The most welcome bird sighting for the serious twitcher (a 'rare bird' sub-group of birdwatchers) is, however, the kiwi—a strange flightless bird that is a cherished national icon in New Zealand. The fragile populations of kiwi and other flightless birds found on the island, such as the weka and dotterels, have started to thrive on Kawau since the establishment of strict environmental protections, delighting the island's small community.

USETT HYTTE

Sjusjøen, Ringsaker, Norway

During the deep Nordic winter, Marianne and Jon Vigtel Hølland wake up in their stylish *hytte* (cabin) in the mountains of Sjusjøen, to a late sunrise. "At this time of year, it's dark in Norway," says Marianne, "so it feels restorative to contemplate the sunrise while drinking our morning coffee."

Later the couple go cross-country skiing. Strapping on wooden skis and following a new path with their dogs Stella and Luna in tow is Marianne's greatest pleasure.

"If it's not too cold, we will stay outside all day and perhaps light a campfire and sit around it until it gets dark and the stars fill the sky. On rare occasions we can see the northern lights. Or if the weather turns bleak, we go inside and warm up in the sauna."

So they can stay outside as much as possible, Marianne and Jon adopt a no-fuss approach to cooking at Usett. A slow-cooked stew is often prepared before the day's outing, hot and ready for their return. "Preferably, we'll add wild foraged ingredients to the meal and accompany it with red wine!" says Marianne.

Located on a hill in the Sjusjøen ski fields, near Lillehammer (scene of the 1994 Winter Olympics), Marianne and Jon's magical mountain getaway was once just a rustic rundown cabin. They purchased it in 2009, site 'unseen', which, in Norwegian translates to *usett*, now the name of the cabin. The goal was to introduce their son, Jesper, and daughter, Ylva, to the great outdoors for "skiing, hiking, getting closer to nature and enjoying valuable family time together."

In the first five years the couple practised simple living in the old cabin, regularly bundling up the children and dogs for the two-hour drive from their home in Oslo. There was no running water, and no roads during winter. "We loved it, and spent almost all weekends during autumn and winter here."

Eventually, water was connected and the road upgraded, but as the small cottage had no space for an acceptable bathroom and kitchen, Marianne and Jon planned an update and a new extension with the help of Marianne's sister, an architect from the office of Benedicte Sund-Mathisen/Suma Arkitektur (see page 286 for details).

With a respectful nod to old mountain barns, a modern extension was added with huge sliding doors on one side opening on to an outdoor terrace. "The materials used in the new build were short-travelled, reused, natural and largely maintenance-free, with extensive use of Norwegian wood—aspen on the inside and ore pine on the outside," says Marianne.

"Now with a good bathroom and sauna, we may no longer be able to call our modern cabin a place for 'simple living', but it is very much 'slow'," says Marianne. "Here we can nurture the body as well as the soul."

All new furniture was built from one-hundred-year-old barn panels, and the leather handles in the kitchen were made from old reindeer reins. The cabin is kept warm with electricity, firewood and underfloor heating. In textural contrast to the polished concrete floor, the lampshades, pillowslips, chair covers and rugs have been felted and knitted by Marianne in wool, largely from Old Norse Spælsau, a breed of sheep.

"The materials used in the build were short-travelled, reused, natural and largely maintenance-free, with extensive use of Norwegian wood—aspen on the inside and ore pine on the outside."

—*Marianne*

"I use wild knitting as a way of contemplating both the nature outside, and the nature within."

—Marianne

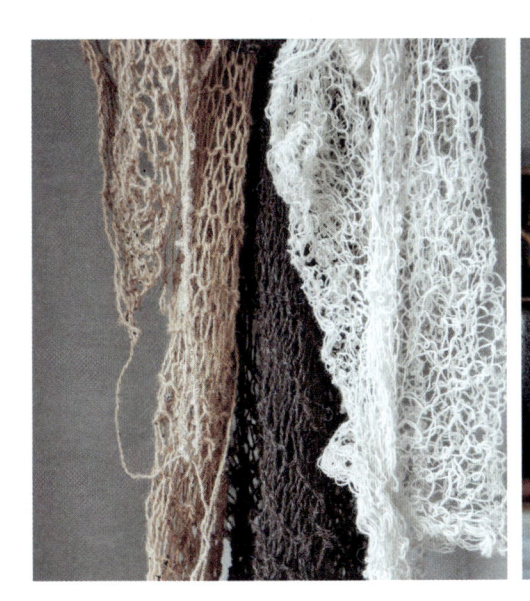

Marianne primarily describes herself as a wild knitter, working as a multidisciplinary designer, author, photographer and mentor through her Slow Design studio practice (see page 286 for details). "My 'slow design' philosophy and aesthetics are influenced by the way I connect to, and observe, nature, but also how it makes me feel," she explains. "I use wild knitting as a way of contemplating both the nature outside, and the nature within," she continues.

The cold-climate landscape yields a variety of colours, shapes and textures that continuously inform Marianne's practice. "On my treks, I collect sticks from different trees to make knitting needles. I will stop for a while, face the pale winter sun and feel its warmth and the strong presence of nature in every cell of me."

"How we choose to build and organise our homes, and the things we choose to surround us, can affect us on several levels," she says. "Environmental inspiration here in the mountains is endless. The snow shifts from light powder to wet and heavy drifts, or freezes into rock-hard ice, then the wind whips it up—nature puts on a never-ending performance."

CROSS-COUNTRY SKIING IN SJUSJØEN

Surrounded by forest and mountain terrain, the ski fields of Sjusjøen are located in eastern Norway. In winter Sjusjøen is popular as a cross-country skiing destination, boasting 350 kilometres (217 miles) of groomed trails that traverse its spectacular pine forests and open country. Sjusjøen is most famously the home to the 54-kilometre-long (33.5-mile-long) Birkebeiner Trail, where one of the world's largest cross-country ski races is held each year. In other seasons, it is also a hiking and water sports mecca, largely due to the natural beauty of the area, which includes Lake Sjusjøen and a number of rivers.

This winter wonderland sees snow falling from November to April, which offers the outdoor enthusiast plenty of options to enjoy the spectacular landscape in ways other than skiing. The icy lake provides opportunities for skating and hockey, but the wintery terrain is where some of the most breathtaking activities take place. Dog-sledding with a team of huskies makes for a thrilling adventure, hurtling deep into the mountains through woodlands and across open country, while a slow ride through whisper-quiet, snow-laden forests on Icelandic horses is nothing short of majestic.

SOL TO SOUL HOUSE

Pioneertown, California, United States

In the Mojave Desert, a stark white minimalist box sits in striking contrast to the dramatic russet amphitheatre of boulders that tower over and curl around it. Ideally positioned in its remote location to inspire creativity and mindfulness, the low-impact dwelling was built as a sanctuary for owner Leslie Longworth to escape her busy life in Los Angeles as a writer and investor.

"My vision for building Sol to Soul was always for it to be a place to slow down, reconnect with nature and the people I love, especially my two teens, Harrison and Lucie. I wanted to be in the moment, to have a space in which to create, write, dream, and just be without any schedule or agenda," she says.

The land on which the smooth white 'getaway' sits never fails to take Leslie's breath away every time she pulls into the driveway after an easy two-and-a-half hour trip from Los Angeles: "Whale Rock behind the house rises up as if from a long-ago sea to greet us and confirm that we have indeed crossed over into the mystical!" she says.

The story of building Sol to Soul began in 2017, when Leslie was on a solo trip to the desert. "It was one of those 'dark night of the soul' moments, and I needed to see stars, lie on the earth, download messages from the universe, and find the courage of the Phoenix to burn myself down and start over," she explains.

"A friend took me to see a large parcel of land in Pioneertown called Gamma Gulch. Everything just felt right," says Leslie.

"My vision for building Sol to Soul was always for it to be a place to slow down, reconnect with nature and the people I love, especially my two teens."

—*Leslie*

Shortly thereafter she contracted Cover, an architectural start-up. The entire process, from design to build took two years (including digging a well, installing septic and electrical, and extensive grading and excavation of giant rock on the site's difficult terrain). The two-bedroom prefabricated home was completed with modern fixtures and finishes, Wolf Sub-Zero appliances, and a state-of-the-art radiant heating and cooling system. To help offset the expense of it, Leslie shares Sol to Soul as a holiday rental (see page 286 for details).

Inside the house, floor-to-ceiling windows frame the boulders. Warm wood and white furniture dominate the space, as well as a Christian Liaigre Opium Daybed that Leslie relocated from her home in Los Angeles and re-covered in a linen the colour of the desert, while outside there are plenty of outdoor dining and lounging options.

A typical day for Leslie and her companions often begins with watching the sunrise, a meditation session, and a cup of coffee. Hiking is often next on the agenda. "The path we take up and over the boulders is never the same. We spend a lot of time sitting on rocks, staring at clouds, and being in awe of everything from the desert colours, clarity of the air and sky, to the desert flora, and fauna like lizards, rabbits, quail and hawks," says Leslie. "I often bring books and my laptop with the intention of writing, but I'm often seduced away from it by the vistas."

In the late afternoon, Leslie and co are found relaxing outside, sometimes cooling off in the tin 'cowboy' bath or warming up in the hot tub. "Dinner may or may not happen," she says. "We're content to eat from a cheese board out by the firepit watching the sunset turn into moon rise. The night sky is filled with stars, and if we are lucky, we can view the Milky Way. It ends with a prayer and ritual offering to the land, and a crystal added to the rock-shaped heart on the property."

Leslie says her favourite part of the desert is what initially captivated her during her first trip to Pioneertown: "the stars, the darkness, the stillness, the silence, for as Jean Baudrillard said, 'The desert is a natural extension of the inner silence of the body'.

"For me, the Mojave strips you of everything that isn't you, takes you back to blood, bone and soul—your inner silence," continues Leslie. "It's like being given a key to reconnect with your essence and know your 'self' as you were before the world got involved. There are also the boulders, which dramatically define the experience in much of the desert. It is said that rocks are the most permanent and stable anchor of the divine, and nowhere do I feel that and the immensity of the universe more than when I am at Sol to Soul."

"We eat out by the firepit watching the sunset turn into moon rise. The night sky is filled with stars, and if we are lucky, we can view the Milky Way."

—*Leslie*

STARGAZING IN THE MOJAVE DESERT

The sparsely populated eastern part of the Mojave Desert, near the old Western-style community of Pioneertown, is known as high desert country due to its elevation of over 1,000 metres (3,280 feet). The rock forms are spectacular, with the granite boulders of Gamma Gulch, in particular, looking like a bag of marbles tossed down from the heavens, landing in a jumble on the towering stone ridges and resting beside the flat-top mesas that dominate the terrain.

Featuring an almost complete absence of humidity, the dry desert environment can only support those plants that require little water, such as cacti, spiky yuccas, Joshua trees and twisted junipers. The majestic boulder-strewn vistas are studded with these sculptural plant forms, and feature spectacular sunsets, faraway coyote howls, and a night sky punctured by billions of stars. Many say the otherworldly landscape inspires a spiritual awakening, beckoning those seeking serendipity to hike though the bulbous landforms to commune with nature. This may account for why the Mojave Desert is known as a mecca for artists, actors, musicians, healers and meditation groups escaping the coastal cities of California for the wild West.

HACHI LILY BUNGALOW

Thủy Biều, Hue, Vietnam

Nestled in a garden of pomelo trees is Hachi Lily, a modern interpretation of the traditional wooden bungalow-style dwellings typical of the culturally rich and bucolic village of Thủy Biều, west of Hue city in central Vietnam.

Positioned on a bend of the Huong (or Perfume River) the village is home to fruit tree groves and tea plantations, as well as many beautiful hundred-year-old ancestral houses hidden within luxuriant gardens and behind fences carved from ornamental trees.

SILAA Architects was commissioned to design and build an architecturally sympathetic retreat for a family of three generations who sought peaceful respite away from the city.

"I always dreamed of living far from the hustle and bustle of the city," says Nguyen Khanh Van, a singer, who enjoys the house with her partner, two children and their grandmother.

Completed in 2021, the simple two-bedroom structure uses natural materials such as wood, stone, gravel and terracotta to reflect the charming architectural styles in neighbouring properties while providing the family with minimalist interiors to promote feelings of calm.

"The main structural frame of the house, as well as the door system and most of the furniture, is made from recycled timber from old buildings. These natural materials, all create a rustic, light colour palette that blends into the natural landscape," says Nguyen Huu Son Duong, principal of SILAA Architects (see page 286 for details).

A stone wall surrounds the bedrooms and bathrooms, creating small private gardens for each room, with seating, shelter and an outdoor shower.

The wide communal living space includes a sofa area, dining table and a kitchenette connected to a verandah that runs along the main side of the house, where a small wooden bridge crosses the water lily pond at the main entrance. "The peaceful atmosphere of the green garden and open space has helped connect the family with the surrounding nature as well as connecting family members with each other," says architect Nguyen Huu Son Duong.

To increase the quality of space inside, an open wooden mezzanine level, accessed via a ladder in the living space, was incorporated as a small library and to provide storage for the family.

To bring in light from above, a skylight has been centred near the ridge of the roof. "The sloped roof has deep eaves that shield and protect the spaces below from the harsh summer sun and heavy rains in winter," says Nguyen Huu Son Duong.

When at Hachi Lily, Nguyen Khanh Van often wakes up early to prepare the breakfast for the children before enjoying a coffee with their grandmother by the water lily pond.

"We can feel the silence of the garden. There are only the sounds of insects and the scent of the pomelo flower."

—*Nguyen Khanh Van*

"After that I start my own work while my mum tends to her small kitchen garden beside the house."

The family matriarch then often prepares a delicious lunch using vegetables from her garden, incorporating many locally bought and produced ingredients, which she serves in the spacious dining area of the house.

"In the afternoon, the wooden mezzanine is a nice place to read a book. It's where you can also touch the pomelo trees near the window while overlooking the common area to see the kids playing," says Nguyen Khanh Van.

Evening, however, is Nguyen Khanh Van's favourite part of the day, because it is then that she can totally relax in the inner garden of the bedroom. "Far into the night, we can feel the silence of the garden. There are only the sounds of insects and the scent of the pomelo flower. Being surrounded by nature, I feel more free and closer to my soul."

SAVOURING THE POMELOS OF THỦY BIỀU

Cradled in a bend of the Huong (Perfume River) in central Vietnam is the ancient village of Thủy Biều. The rustic settlement is surrounded by rice fields and hidden by lush gardens of tropical flowers and fruit, bamboo stands, and groves of citrus trees, with the pomelo, a type of very large grapefruit being the most common.

The pomelo in this part of the country is called Thanh Trà and is a popular crop grown by more than 800 households. Every spring, the village is filled with the fragrance of the white flower of the pomelo and in autumn the ripe fruit is ready to be picked. Due to the proximity to the river and fertile soil in which it grows, the pomelo's flavour is described as semisweet and slightly sour. Its skin and pith are thick and aromatic but these are best peeled away so the segments can be eaten raw like an orange. Pomelo is also used to add a tangy flavour to a salad, or the citrus pulp is mixed with grilled squid and spicy fish sauce for a savoury dish common in Thủy Biều food stalls during the harvest season.

THE RUSTICS

Evoking the simple life, these rustic retreats provide their owners with a connection to a rural past while fostering in them a renewed appreciation for the surrounding natural environment of woodlands, fields and farmlands. Whether found near prehistoric pathways, old stone ruins or on the outskirts of an ancient hamlet, these centuries-old homes have been restored and sympathetically remodelled with traditional building methods and materials. Inside, reimagined interior layouts produce elegant living spaces that often feature decorative references to the home's agrarian, ancestral or folkloric past. These retreats offer the inhabitants calming spaces in which to relax, reflect and reset.

LA FERMETTE DU MERLE

Crux-la-Ville, Burgundy, France

In the peaceful and verdant farmlands of Nièvre in Burgundy, stands La Fermette du Merle, a sweet nineteenth-century farmhouse near the hamlet of Crux-la-Ville. With its pastel-blue window shutters and distressed stone walls covered by rambling pink roses, the *fermette* (small farmhouse) is not only picture-perfect but also ideally positioned on the crest of a hill to take advantage of pretty views of rolling hills, winding roads and forests as far as the eye can see.

The farmhouse is owned by Morgane van Liere and Arvid Niemeijer, a Hilversum-based couple (she's Dutch/French, he's Dutch), who had become disenchanted by the high prices of property in the city. Their solution to owning a house required creative thinking outside the (urban) box. As Arvid says, "It started with a week's holiday in Burgundy …"

"We bought a holiday house in the French countryside just a couple of days before the first COVID-19 lockdown in 2020, got the key in August 2020, and started small restoration and redecoration works," says Morgane.

Since interior design is a passion of Morgane's, and the energetic Arvid likes to build and create, the first phase of the restoration project was completed within a year. "It was important for us that we retain the authentic character of the house, working mainly with old or rural materials, while keeping the interiors bright and adding modern comforts," says Morgane.

"We liked the old kitchen but updated it by painting the cabinets. We kept the old tiles on the living room and bedroom floors but bought a modern couch and new bed. We sourced other furniture at *brocante* (flea markets) or bought them at secondhand shops. We also renewed the roof, choosing new 'old style' tiles. It's all about finding the balance between authenticity and comfort," says Morgane.

"We don't have a television, as we are trying to disconnect from our busy lives in the city. But we do like to listen to music or read," says Arvid. Although, he then realises, "there won't be much time for that now. "Our son Mathieu was born just before Christmas 2021," he beams.

In the warmer months Morgane and Arvid like to spend time in the garden, having their coffee in the morning sun or evening drinks on the terrace (Morgane prefers a white Burgundy). In good weather, the couple adventure further afield, cooling off in the Etang du Merle (Blackbird Pond), a swimming hole just five-minutes' drive away, or hiking in the cool forests of Le Morvan nature park.

"It was important for us that we retain the authentic character of the house, working mainly with old or rural materials, while keeping the interiors bright and adding modern comforts."

—*Morgane*

"The region itself is not so populated, but there are some small villages. It's more a place for people who seek stillness."

—*Morgane*

Every couple of months, the couple spend a week or two in their French abode, and were bunking there during the pandemic to work from home. Sometimes friends join them on their French sojourn, and to celebrate together they set up dinner tables outside under a large nut tree festooned with lanterns. More recently, they have allowed paying guests to rent the farmhouse on a weekly basis during the summer season (see page 286 for details).

La Fermette du Merle is not in a French village, town or even famous tourist destination but in a sparsely populated region. "The property is an escape for people who seek stillness, and who want to observe nature, says Morgane. "From our 6,000-square-metre (1.5-acre) garden, we often see farmers' sheep in our meadow, little owls in the trees and sometimes encounter a fox or deer, and we can look out over fields to the woodlands of the national park of Le Morvan. It's bliss."

CYCLING THROUGH THE MORVAN REGIONAL NATURAL PARK

Nestled halfway between Paris and Lyon in the heart of Burgundy is the Morvan Regional Natural Park: 285,000 hectares (704,250 acres) of mountains, woodlands, lakes, rivers and traditional farmlands. The highest peak is Le Haut-Folin, standing at an altitude of 901 metres (2,956 feet). Visitors to the park hike, walk, cycle or horse-ride through the mountains and forests, or go swimming, fishing, sailing or paddling on one of six calm and beautiful lakes. In winter it is possible to enjoy cross-country skiing, thanks to 40 kilometres (25 miles) of marked-out tracks.

The park is rich in flora and fauna. In spring, primroses, hyacinth and wild daffodils bloom. In summer, wild strawberries, blackberries and raspberries are widespread, and in autumn, mushrooms emerge from the moist groundcover of the forest. In the air, hawks, falcons and eagles circle high in search of prey, and there are many species of owl that appear at night. By day, numerous delightful woodland birds like the finch, wren or swallow are active. The park is also home to many small creatures, like rabbits and hares, squirrels and mice, polecats and weasels, but larger animals are common, too, such as deer, wild boars, foxes and badgers.

AGAPAKI STUDIO

Agapi, Tinos, Greece

Perched on a rocky hillside on the island of Tinos is the small mountain village of Agapi—a tiny settlement that owes its name to its religious patron saint, Agapitos, meaning 'love' in Greek. Secreted within the village network of old winding stone alleyways and stairs, a small white studio dwelling stood waiting to be discovered by couple Alexandra Papadimouli and Peter Grivas, city-dwellers from Athens who had been searching for three years to realise their dream to own an island bolthole.

"After lots of village-hopping we finally got lucky and discovered an almost hidden 'For Sale' sign in Agapi. It was perfect," says Alexandra. "My husband Peter is the reason I fell in love with Tinos. He insisted on taking me there, since it was his mother's birthplace."

They discovered the little house together, bought it, renovated it, and now enjoy it as often as they can leave the mainland. "We visit a few times a year, while during the summer I try to stay for more than three months in a row and work from there," says Alexandra, relieved to have at last found respite from the urban pressures of living in a modern apartment in downtown Athens.

"When I take a stroll outside my village, I see the valley full of stone wall fences, small churches and, of course, the island's famed dovecotes. I also come across goats and cows and other small animals grazing, smell the thyme and oregano in the air and discover the caper and other plants that grow in the area. All of this influences my work."

—*Alexandra*

The couple's urban and island homes couldn't be more different. Their roomy Athens apartment is in a neighbourhood crammed with apartment blocks, cars, noise, and narrow streets, while the island home is quite the opposite: a thick-walled stone studio abode of just 30 square metres (98 square feet) set in a tranquil ancient village that features Cycladic town planning. In Agapi, houses are traditionally built one upon the other offering protection and climatic control while forming a labyrinth of delightful passageways that only people, cats and the occasional donkey can navigate.

This way of life influences Alexandra's artwork (see page 287 for details). "My main source of inspiration comes from the island of Tinos," she says. "The creative process for me begins while exploring the island in order to discover architectural shapes and natural elements that can be later recreated as minimalist shapes in my art pieces. I create art because it is my way of escaping reality, a way of breathing in village life and exhaling everyday city life."

When Alexandra takes a stroll outside her village, she sees a valley full of stone wall fences, small churches and, of course, the island's famed dovecotes, also known as pigeon houses. "I also come across goats and cows and other small animals grazing, smell the thyme and oregano in the air, and discover the caper and other plants that grow in the area. All of this influences my work."

The found materials and colours of the surrounding landscapes informed the refurbishment of the studio, too. "After restoring the studio, our first decision was that white and stone-grey tones would dominate the space, so it bonded with the traditional Cycladic style," says Alexandra. "Bulkier furniture, such as the bed and the sofa, were built-in according to the local interior architecture, and we painted the smaller pieces (office, table, cabinets) in black to create contrast. We love natural tones and materials for the decorative elements like throws, pillows, ceramics, etc. The only items with colour you will see in Agapaki will be on the walls: the artworks!"

"After restoring the studio, our first decision was that white and stone-grey tones would dominate the space, so it bonded with the traditional Cycladic style."

—*Alexandra*

"Our favourite place in our home is the private balcony!" says Alexandra. "It's where I spend most of the day when I come here alone to paint. When Peter's with me, we eat, read and entertain friends here. Later we'll recline on the built-in sofa, gazing at the stars."

Depending on the weather and their mood, Alexandra and Peter might drive to the beach, ten minutes away, or explore another of the small island villages. "Almost every day includes a short afternoon nap (a luxury we don't have in the city)," says Alexandra. "In the evening, Peter and I either go for a stroll in the village that most often ends in the square at the small taverna, or find ourselves on a friend's balcony for *raki* (local spirit) and chat. Our island life is always relaxing and often inspiring. It was exactly what we had been craving."

ADMIRING THE DOVECOTES OF TINOS

Dovecotes, also known as pigeon houses, are scattered across the Cycladic islands, the most impressive of which are found on the island of Tinos. There are over a thousand still standing, in various states of repair, and date from the seventeenth and eighteenth centuries. Featuring striking ornate façades of various geometric patterns of circles, triangles, diamonds and squares, which are conspicuously arranged on the upper storey to encourage pigeons to roost there, these imposing buildings were built using local stone by farmers for housing and breeding pigeons.

Historically, pigeon meat has been prized in the Cyclades, and on Tinos there is the possibility to eat pigeon stew, although it is no longer common. The buildings were also a depository for pigeon droppings, which the farmers collected to use as fertiliser on their fields. Inside, the ground floor was used as a storeroom for farming goods, agricultural tools or to harbour animals or people caught on the hills in poor weather. Most of the Tinos dovecotes are concentrated in the more fertile central area of the island, which includes the hills and the valleys of Agapi.

TRULLO STELLA MARE

Lamie di Olimpia, Puglia, Italy

Many of us spend hours on the internet indulging in 'property porn', looking for our dream home or a holiday escape, but you have to seriously raise the bar to match the exhaustive search undertaken by seasoned investigative journalist Paola Totaro if you are to find the 'perfect' Italian getaway.

"One year, we spent the whole summer looking at properties," says Paola, who left no 'virtual' crumbling stone unturned in the hills of Puglia to find a *trullo*—a traditional dry-stone conical hut with a corbelled roof unique to the Itria Valley. "We found ours on the internet and flew from London to see it. My husband Robert fell in love with the place straight away. It was high on a hill with 180-degree views of the Adriatic coastline." The fact that the property was literally a pile of rocks didn't stop Paola and Robert purchasing the historic ruin on a 5,000-square-metre (1.25-acre) plot.

After a major restoration (detailed in Paola's blog, see page 287 for details), the couple were determined any updates to the home would remain faithful to the structures' humble origins as small shelters for farmers during harvest season. They kept the interiors simple, beyond adding the necessities such as running water and power. The floors are a poured and coloured concrete (originally there would have been stone directly on the earth), furnishings are agrarian in style and there is lots of wood and decorative nods to an uncomplicated life of centuries past.

Paola's lovingly collected vintage finds animate the *trullo*'s interior, from simple seats around her grandparents' kitchen table to the wooden kitchen utensil frame that hangs on a wall by the stove. "I wanted the spaces to feel as rustic as they would have when they were home to both humans and animals," says Paola, "so you will find them decorated with milking stools, old wooden hay forks, mismatched cutlery and enamel candle holders."

The *trullo* grounds are an ongoing project: "We are building a garden out of rough, tough, long-abandoned land. There are lots of figs, stone fruit and olive trees but they've taken time to re-nurture; and we are re-wilding and planting lots of bee-friendly bushes and Mediterranean (and appropriate Australian) plants that are heat tolerant and can do without too much water."

Built in the late 1700s, the *trullo* is surrounded by olive trees and close to protected woodlands known as the Selva di Fasano. To the west is the Valle d'Itria (Itria Valley), which is dotted with spectacular whitewashed hillside towns, among them Alberobello and Ostuni, although the closest medieval tourist town is pretty Locorotondo.

Since the region is renowned for its food, Paola and Robert often head into a village to buy fresh produce or to a farmers' market before a stop at their favourite café. "I love cooking and tend to stick to simple, Italian dishes and salads when we are home," says Paola.

"I wanted the spaces to feel as rustic as they would have when they were home to both humans and animals, so you will find them decorated with milking stools, old wooden hay forks, mismatched cutlery and enamel candle holders."

—*Paola*

Paola and Robert have made many local friends. "Our neighbours often welcome our arrival with homemade food. We help them pick their grapes, they pick our olives, and we often share meals," says Paola.

Sometimes the couple invite English friends to holiday with them, although, due to COVID-19 travel restrictions, they are still waiting for their Australian family to visit, including three adult children (the fourth and youngest is in the United Kingdom). The *trullo* is also rented out when Paola and Robert are back in London (see page 287 for details).

When at the *trullo* the couple rarely stop writing. Paola, who was born in Italy and raised in Australia, is a writer, a former Europe correspondent for the *Sydney Morning Herald* and the *Age*, Melbourne, and a former President of the Foreign Press Association in London, while husband Robert Wainwright is an ex-journalist and author of fourteen books. Both always have a project on the go.

"You will often find us with our laptops, under a tree or by the pool—wherever there is shade—typing away!" says Paola, who is currently working on a PhD, writing a book of historical nonfiction about a French perfumer set in nineteenth-century Naples. "When my brain needs a rest, I knit and crochet—I made a couple of blankets for the *trullo*!"

When the couple met twenty-five years ago as newspaper journalists and eventually wed, the rings they exchanged were decorated with starfish. This symbol of love ultimately inspired the name of Trullo Stella Mare (which means 'Star/Sea'). "I had a dream about a starfish, which was somehow connected to a slow, reassuring heartbeat and, weirdly, this stayed with me and gave me courage to embark on a new life chapter in London, our marriage, and later, the *trullo* project," says Paola. "The name also fits our holiday home because at night we are surrounded by stars, and we can always see the sea!"

"We breakfast outside under the pergola, and either sit by the pool and read or plan a day at the beach twenty minutes' drive away."

—*Paola*

ENJOYING THE FOODS OF THE ITRIA VALLEY

Nestled in the heart of Puglia is Itria Valley. Fringed by the stunning Adriatic coastline, the Itria countryside is dominated by groves of olive, almond and fig trees, numerous vineyards and pretty hill towns featuring the whitewashed *trullo* houses typical of the region. The rolling hills are criss-crossed by winding country lanes, dry-stone walls and rich farmland that produces some of the country's best produce.

Food is at the heart of the region's culture, from olive oil and wine to seafood. Particular to the area are pastas, such as *orecchiette* and *strangolapreti* (aka priest chokers), freshly made cheeses, such as *ricotta*, *mozzarella*, *burrata* and *cacio*, and meats such as handmade sausages, *capocollo* ham, and *bombette*—small, tender rolls of meat stuffed with various cheeses and salami, which are chargrilled by a butcher while you wait (often in a courtyard trattoria restaurant adjoining the shop) and served with a simple green salad and a dry white Locorotondo wine. Of course, the baked goods and pastries are memorable, too. Served with a coffee, sometimes sweetened with almond syrup, there are such delights as almond *biscotti cegliesi*, cream-filled *pasticciotto*, or fried savoury dough balls called *pettole*.

YUI VALLEY KOMINKA

Tamatori, Fujieda, Shizuoka, Japan

Nestled in a peaceful valley surrounded by bamboo groves, green tea plantations and mountains in central Japan is a hundred-year-old country house owned by Daisuke Kajiyama (Dai) and his Israeli wife, Hila Gay Kajiyama. They call it Yui Valley house.

"We love the spiritual feeling of the word *yui*, which in Japanese means 'circle' or 'connection'," says Dai. "The house provides a connection to where we are in nature, to the people we meet and to ourselves."

Located halfway between the bustling metropolis of Tokyo and Kyoto, Yui Valley house sits beside a crystal-clear stream that flows through the rural village of Fujieda, where in nearby Okabe there are remnants of the Tokaido—an ancient road that once connected the shogun's feudal stronghold of Edo (Tokyo) to imperial Kyoto.

Dai and Hila met years ago in Nepal while they were each travelling through Asia. They longed to be together, but where? On a trip back to Japan with Dai, Hila fell in love with his country and so the decision was made that Japan would be their base, returning to Hila's homeland, Israel, as often as possible. However, with the events of recent years impacting travel, that hasn't been possible, so the couple have hunkered down in the countryside, sharing their restored *kominka* (a traditional wooden house) with paying guests (see page 287 for details).

The *kominka* had been abandoned for seven years before the couple rescued it. With the help of a carpenter friend, and support enlisted by exchanging bed and meals for labour from young volunteers visiting Japan on a budget, they repaired it. "Our strategy was not to change the house much," says Dai. "Just fix where it's broken and make it more comfortable without damaging the authentic and *wabi-sabi* feel, that is, the aesthetic of imperfection of the house."

Hila says there is so much to love about Yui Valley house: "Sliding paper doors open to pretty views allowing a connection between the inside and outside. It's like living in another era. Everything feels authentic and untainted. For example, our drinking water comes from underground. It's so clean and tasty. When you're in bed on a futon on the tatami floor, you fall asleep to the sound of the river and you wake up to the sound of birds."

Hila is a keen gardener. She helps with planting organic rice and has perfected the art of sourdough bread making. The couple usually start the day with coffee and Hila's freshly baked bread, eating it in the garden while enjoying the view. "We will cook together nice food for lunch and dinner. Maybe I will bake a cake," says Hila. "Sometimes one of our neighbours brings freshly harvested vegetables, or one of the grandmothers will bring pickles she made—these visits really brighten our day."

"In summer, we can cool off in the river next to the house," says Dai. "It is beautiful, clean rainwater, always running with tiny fish."

When Dai is not harvesting the bamboo shoots that emerge in early spring in the village groves or cutting the towering plants down later in the year, he takes time to do bamboo weaving (*takezaiku*), a craft Dai has mostly taught himself.

"There's a lot to working with bamboo," says Dai, "from taking care of the forest itself, harvesting the bamboo, then treating, splitting, drying and preparing the strings for weaving. The fun part is when you start to weave, and then … as the shape is appearing, you can look up and see the bamboo forest at same time."

"Coming here makes us happy in so many ways," says Hila, who while missing Israel can't complain about the haven she has landed in. "The country house itself is so charming, the nature around it is beautiful, and we love to host and meet like-minded people and share with them the joy of this house. We feel so safe when we're here, and with our neighbours, none of us needs to lock our house doors—we care for and trust each other."

"Sliding paper doors open to pretty views allowing a connection between the inside and outside. It's like living in another era."

—*Hila*

"There's a lot to working with bamboo, from taking care of the forest itself, harvesting the bamboo, then treating, splitting, drying and preparing the strings for weaving."

—*Daisuke*

WANDERING THROUGH THE BAMBOO OF TAMATORI

In the bamboo forests of Tamatori, deep in the mountains of Shizuoka Prefecture, the tall, slender stalks of the 'giant' bamboo species sway in the slightest breeze. Even in the strongest winds, giant bamboo bends but never breaks, and yet grows to a towering height, between 10 and 20 metres (33 and 66 feet) in a single growing season lasting a few months. The Japanese believe the strength of bamboo (called *take*) teaches them to stand upright, while its flexibility teaches them to adapt to the harshest circumstances.

Bamboo can be found everywhere in Japan, and while the groves are serene places to walk through, the plant has many uses. Come spring, its tender shoots, called *takenoko*, are dug up and eaten as a delicacy and the cut poles are used widely as a material for construction: for scaffolding, in walls, as fences. Bamboo is also used to beautify Japanese gardens and interiors or made into traditional items, such as tea ceremony utensils, chopsticks, flutes or fans. When stripped into lengths, bamboo is woven into basketry to form a vast array of simple household and religious products, from platters to serve tempura to vases for displaying ikebana flower arrangements.

FINCA ALFABIA

Ruberts, Mallorca, Spain

While the island of Mallorca is perhaps best known for its beaches and mountains, it is in the lesser-explored wine country in the centre of the island where soulmates Tyson Strang and Tatiana Baibabaeva, founders of the interior design team Terra Coll Home, realised their dream of owning an ancient stone house in the Mediterranean. "We searched in this region to immerse ourselves in a more authentic experience of rural Mallorcan life," says Tyson, a former assistant principal and literature teacher in New York City who is also now a practising ceramicist.

"We envisioned living purposefully and simply, connecting to the land and the past, in an old home built with honest and sustainable materials, and spending our time making beautiful things. We wanted something homey and escapist at the same time," says Tyson.

The couple soon bought a 300-year-old *finca* (traditional farmhouse) set on 3.5 hectares (9 acres) surrounded by rolling pasture and protected forests of Aleppo pines, holm oaks, and wild olives. Both Tyson and Tatiana, who is also a ceramicist as well as a fashion designer (born in Kyrgyzstan, raised in Russia, and more lately a New Yorker), planned to hole up while the pandemic afflicted their home city of New York, subletting their penthouse apartment on the Upper West Side to begin work restoring the *finca*, while giving their toddler son Ferrán a taste of a free-spirited life.

They also decided to design and reform the *finca* themselves, albeit with help from stonemasons, carpenters, and iron workers from nearby villages. "The feeling of accomplishment that comes from such personal investment in a project is very powerful," says Tyson.

Tyson and Tatiana's love for the original structure meant the materials used in the restoration are almost all local and sustainable; hardly anything is manufactured or prefabricated. "The sinks, for example, have been chiselled from stones found in the yard," says Tatiana. "The pergola we built near the pool is made entirely from the trunks and branches of trees we removed to install the pool."

The interior finishes and décor had to be functional, handmade, practical, and genuine. Furniture had to be constructed to fit spaces according to need. Fixtures and design elements had to be made locally or, even better, found on the land. "We wanted all colours to reflect the nature outside, with a purposeful absence of bright colours inside, and instead with a focus on textures and finishes." The result is that nearly every surface of the house has become "a tactile and earthy experience".

About seven years ago, Tyson and Tatiana began a small ceramics business in New York as an outlet for their creativity. "At first it was a diversion, and we loved the sentiment of eating and drinking from dinnerware we had made ourselves," says Tyson. Through their work on the *finca*, that diversion soon launched a new career path as interior designers. "After all, if drinking from your own mug brings a certain satisfaction, the experience of preparing that tea in a kitchen you designed and built yourself is a much more rewarding experience."

"We came to think of it as 'living well'," says Tyson, who has set up a studio on the *finca*'s grounds. "We wanted to spend a lot of our time surrounded by beauty, doing things we loved, and making things that mattered to us. Terra Coll Home is the name we have given to our creative partnership, which sprang from the idea about where and how we wanted to spend our time." (See page 287 for details.)

The *finca*, far removed from the bright lights and big city of New York, takes, according to Tyson, about sixteen hours door-to-door via road, air and sea. The little family now get to enjoy a dual life, as Tyson says, finding the peace and privacy they craved in a creative retreat where living in the slow lane is perhaps the only rule.

"Whatever we added to the house had to be hard to distinguish from what was already there, which meant that materials, techniques, and mood had to be consistent with a 300-year-old farmhouse."

—*Tyson*

When the family summer in Mallorca, the days start early. They often work on one unfinished house project or another, then by 11am the sun becomes unbearably hot and they retreat to the pool for a swim and sit in the shade. "We'll eat a salad, usually a traditional *trampo* with tomatoes, peppers, and onions gifted by our neighbour, Pedro, then siesta until 2pm or so," says Tyson. "Then it's off to a secluded cove, either alone or with friends, which invariably involves a hike through ancient olive groves and pines down to the sea. After sunset, it's back home for some grilled local lamb or rabbit and the joy of outdoor dining on a refreshing summer's night."

In winter, the couple get up early as usual to play with Ferrán but linger around the kitchen over coffee and tea. "The sun comes over the treeline around 10am and sunlight streams through the windows and doors. This is usually the time we start on whatever project we are doing, such as ceramics, gardening or a little more restoration work," says Tatiana.

Restoring the *finca* has fuelled Tyson and Tatiana's creative passion over the last few years, both in the design and construction processes. "We have learned a lot, and we get a powerful sense of fulfilment from being so deeply involved in the creation of our vision," says Tatiana. "The experience is everything we were hoping it would be when we bought the *finca*. It has not only become our country escape but an ideal creative sanctuary for us, too."

"We wanted to spend a lot of our time surrounded by beauty, doing things we loved, and making things that mattered to us."

—*Tyson*

CLIFF WALKING IN THE PENÍNSULA DE LLEVANT NATURE PARK

The island of Mallorca is well known for its stunning beaches, laid-back cantinas, wineries and fresh produce farms, but it also has some spectacular nature parks. Renowned for its hilly terrain, Península de Llevant Nature Park is located in the northeast of Mallorca. It was declared a national park in 2002 and covers 1,671 hectares (4,129 acres) of protected landscape, much of which includes the Artà mountain range. The habitats are diverse, with vast expanses of scrubland featuring Mauritanian grass and the European fan palm, but there are also forests of holm oak, wild olive trees and pine trees, as well as unspoilt beaches and streams.

Hiking trails criss-cross the park, some of which hug the dramatic coastline of the peninsula, where rare birds such as the peregrine falcon, booted eagle, Audouin's gull, European shag and red kite roost in clifftop crags. There are also numerous Mediterranean tortoise colonies, specifically the Hermann's tortoise, which is part of a breeding program, as well as animals such as the Algerian hedgehog, the genet, the pine marten, and the Balearic green toad, while herds of Mallorcan cows, sheep, donkeys and wild goats roam even in remote areas.

LITTLE HARP COTTAGE

Old Radnor, Powys, Wales, United Kingdom

The sense of connecting to an ancient past is appreciated by Albert Hill when walking the trails around his historic but stylish Welsh holiday home in Old Radnor, a tiny hamlet that sits atop a hill overlooking a valley in which neolithic remains of a prehistoric tribal gathering place have been discovered. For it is on this ancient Celtic land that his seventeenth-century stone cottage, Little Harp, was built. "From our position on the ridge, there are amazing views over the green Radnor Valley where you watch the weather roll in and birds of prey swooping in the sky. It feels so ancient and unchanged," says Albert.

Undulating farmlands now cover the land, their paddocks separated by dry-stone walls, but instead of Druid circles, old churches are now the dominant places of worship in the villages. Opposite Little Harp cottage, for example, is the imposing fifteenth-century St Stephen's Church, constructed in Perpendicular Gothic style on the site of a sixth-century church. Nearby is an old pub, the Harp Inn, which occupies a fifteenth-century longhouse, but there are few other dwellings in the hamlet.

Little Harp is an old Welsh farmhouse Albert and his wife Ciara bought in 2020 from a listing on themodernhouse.com, which showcases some of the best homes for sale in the United Kingdom and also features the coolest homes around the world in the site's magazine. Albert is cofounder of both this site and Inigo (historic houses of the United Kingdom), and is passionate about architecture. "I am obsessed with homes, their owners and their histories!" says Albert, a former long-term design editor of *Wallpaper** magazine. (See page 287 for details, including rental.)

"The stone walls and floors and wooden beams created a lot of the appeal. We gave the home a bit of colour and intrigue with stylish furniture, and some of our twentieth-century art collection, as we are big art lovers!"

—*Albert*

It was the inherent beauty of the cottage that first attracted Albert and Ciara. "The stone walls and floors and wooden beams created a lot of the appeal," says Albert. "We really liked the way the previous owner, Justine Cook, had refurbished it, so when we bought it, we didn't do a great deal other than to give the home a bit of colour and intrigue with stylish furniture, and to hang some of our twentieth-century art collection there as we are big art lovers! A recent wooden extension was kept simple and humble but is a more contemporary build."

Newly installed underfloor heating downstairs and two wood-burning stoves keep the three-bedroom cottage cosy in winter. The house is surrounded by a small garden on three sides. At the front is a farmer's track that leads to a neighbouring field, which is often filled with sheep (as are most of the nearby fields). Albert and Ciara take their two children, Arlo and Jackson, and dog, Rusty, hiking on most occasions they are at their country getaway. If they are lucky, they might encounter the wild ponies of the greater Wye River Valley.

"We love going to the nearby town of Kington, which has great local shops and a weekly market attended by local producers," says Albert. "If we are at the cottage at the right time, our plum tree is heavy with fruit, so we make crumble; if not, we visit a local chocolate maker, Alexandra Pechabadens, who makes her chocolate by hand. It's the best chocolate in the United Kingdom!"

"Luckily our children love coming to our Welsh hideaway, so we try to go there as often as possible to get a bit of breathing space away from work and school and the crowded roads of the southeast of England where we live in Surrey, which is about a three hours' drive from Wales," says Albert. "I often go on my own, and so does Ciara, as a rare opportunity to get a bit of peace and quiet by oneself!"

On these solo trips, Albert takes Rusty to accompany him on his country walks. "I also love waking up in the morning and seeing the trees and sky from the bedroom window. It's a rejuvenating experience."

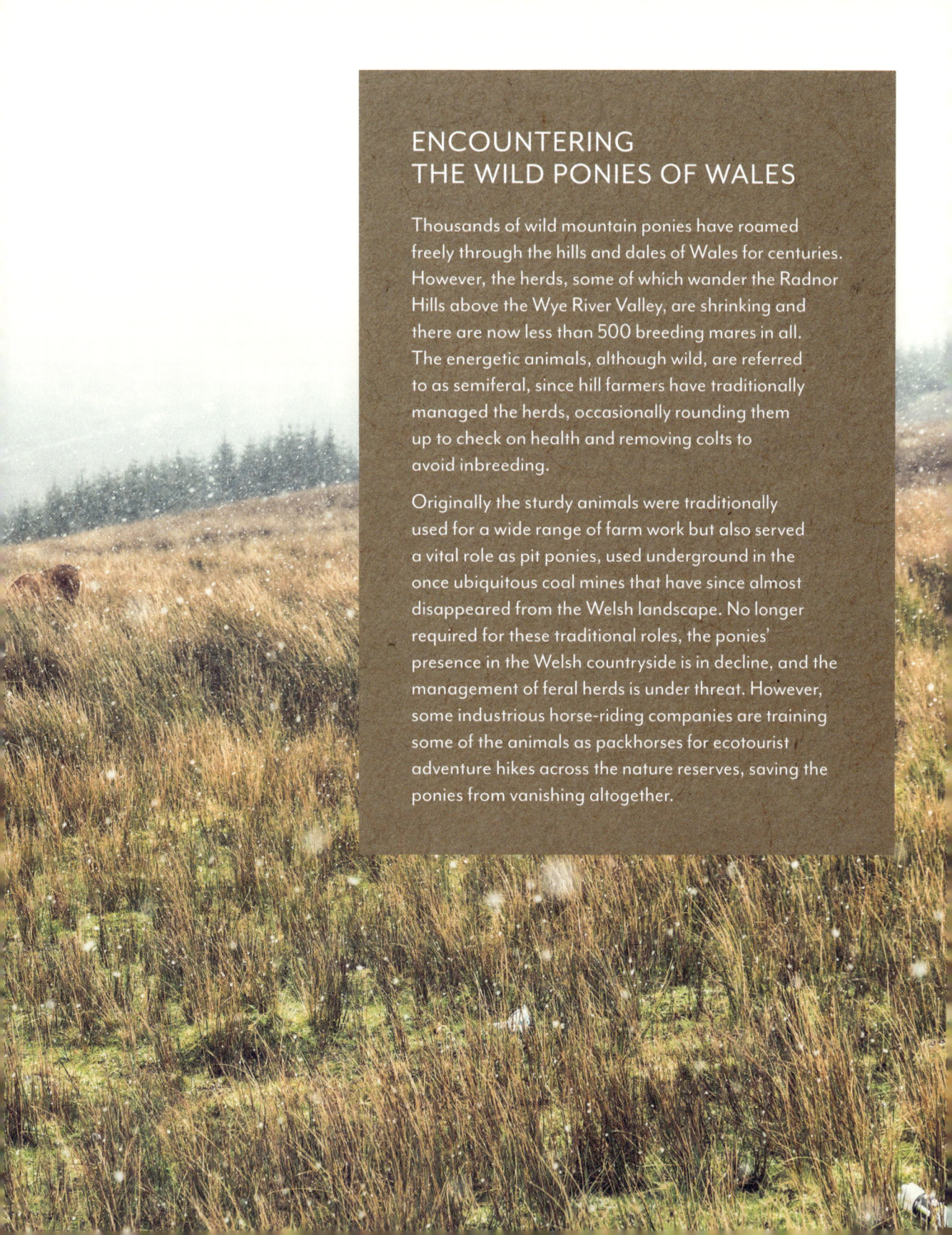

ENCOUNTERING
THE WILD PONIES OF WALES

Thousands of wild mountain ponies have roamed freely through the hills and dales of Wales for centuries. However, the herds, some of which wander the Radnor Hills above the Wye River Valley, are shrinking and there are now less than 500 breeding mares in all. The energetic animals, although wild, are referred to as semiferal, since hill farmers have traditionally managed the herds, occasionally rounding them up to check on health and removing colts to avoid inbreeding.

Originally the sturdy animals were traditionally used for a wide range of farm work but also served a vital role as pit ponies, used underground in the once ubiquitous coal mines that have since almost disappeared from the Welsh landscape. No longer required for these traditional roles, the ponies' presence in the Welsh countryside is in decline, and the management of feral herds is under threat. However, some industrious horse-riding companies are training some of the animals as packhorses for ecotourist adventure hikes across the nature reserves, saving the ponies from vanishing altogether.

DESERT CABIN

Joshua Tree, California, United States

An eclectic mix of desert dwellers, survivalists, artists and musicians forms the community that initially attracted Kathrin and Brian Smirke to the dry wilderness of eastern California. The idea of connecting with like-minded people and escaping to a bolthole under a star-studded desert sky became increasingly fixated in the couple's minds, who normally live by the sea in northern California on the Mendocino coast. The plan was to buy and renovate a run-down desert shack that they could escape to when time permitted, renting it out to others in-between times.

"We wanted to create a getaway that would be a personal escape from our busy city lives and as a place to re-energise in solace under the desert sky," says Kathrin.

Years ago, on a weekend away to Joshua Tree National Park, Kathrin and Brian found a derelict cabin that they purchased and more or less rebuilt, gutting the place, then remodelling it to create a boho vibe. They called their little desert oasis Cabin Cabin Cabin! (See page 287 for details.)

"Our aim was to stick to a budget on the big expenses, and be as creative as possible with the decoration and design," says Kathrin.

Located just outside the western entrance to the Joshua Tree National Park, the little one-bedroom abode has a rather plain white exterior but inside the white rooms have been curated and decorated with care, displaying prized southwestern trinkets, including crystals and dreamcatchers, to ensure nothing but good vibrations.

"We added colour and texture to the home by decorating it with colourful kilim-covered cushions, Navajo-style rugs and blankets, macramé planters, and terracotta-potted cactus," says Kathrin. "We polished the concrete floors to keep the interiors clean and cool, and offset this with rustic wooden beams and panels, some of which we salvaged from the demolition."

After a long day hiking to Coyote Hole Canyon or trekking in Joshua Tree National Park, Kathrin or Brian often take a long soak in the claw-foot outdoor bath while the other flops in the hammock under trees nearby. As Brian is a musician turned real estate developer and Kathrin is a glass artist-cum-stylist, time spent in the unspoiled environment inspires their creativity as well as their spirituality.

"It's really such an incredible feeling out here in Joshua Tree," says Kathrin. "I especially love it when friends join us on a walk and we find a rocky platform to sit on and meditate. You can't help but feel small in the expanse of desert that stretches out before you but connected to the earth and each other at the same time. Our desert cabin is a nature lover's dream getaway, inviting us to unplug, enjoy the outdoors—and admire the surrounding Joshua trees, of course."

"We wanted to create a getaway that would be a personal escape from our busy city lives and as a place to re-energise in solace under the desert sky."

—*Kathrin*

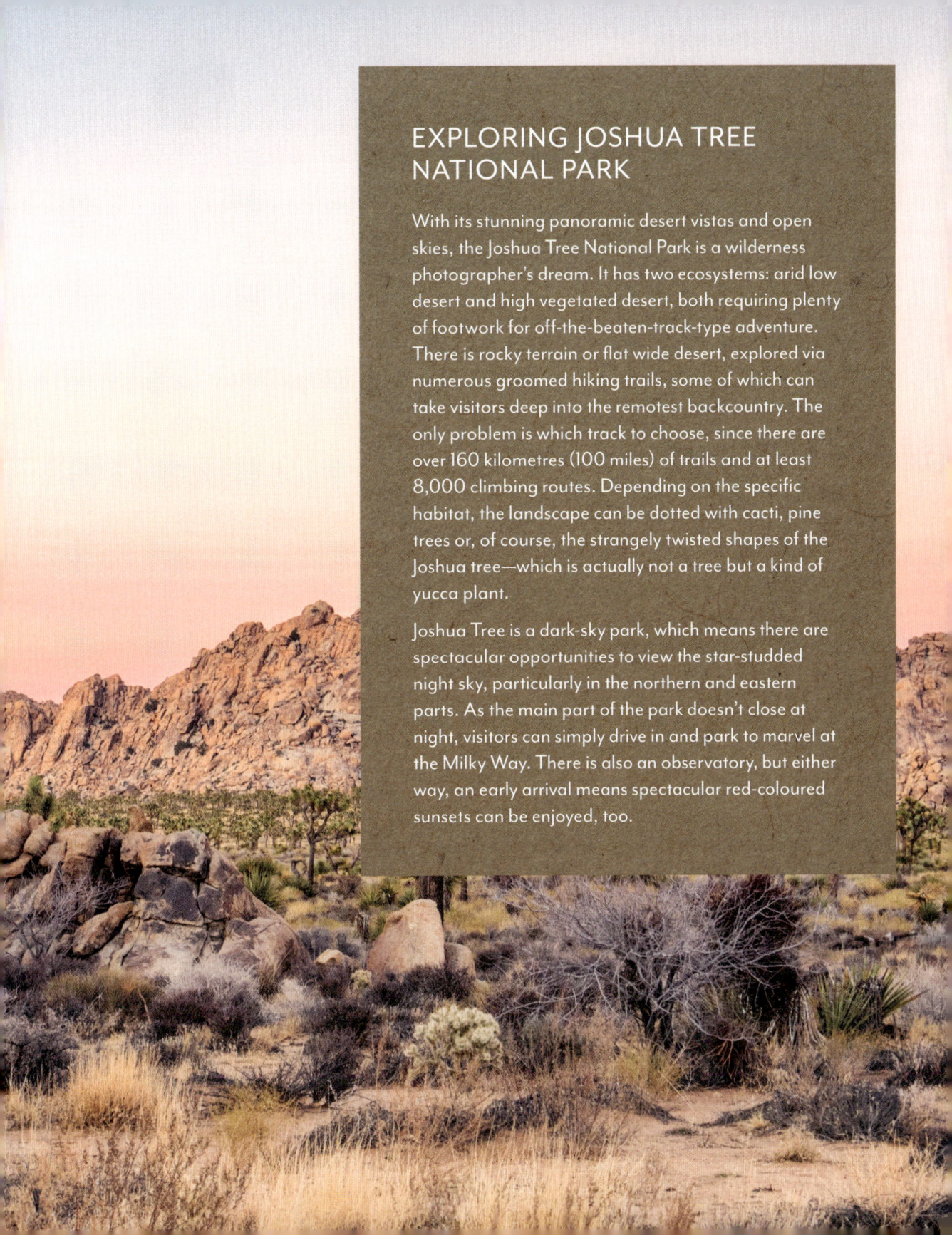

EXPLORING JOSHUA TREE NATIONAL PARK

With its stunning panoramic desert vistas and open skies, the Joshua Tree National Park is a wilderness photographer's dream. It has two ecosystems: arid low desert and high vegetated desert, both requiring plenty of footwork for off-the-beaten-track-type adventure. There is rocky terrain or flat wide desert, explored via numerous groomed hiking trails, some of which can take visitors deep into the remotest backcountry. The only problem is which track to choose, since there are over 160 kilometres (100 miles) of trails and at least 8,000 climbing routes. Depending on the specific habitat, the landscape can be dotted with cacti, pine trees or, of course, the strangely twisted shapes of the Joshua tree—which is actually not a tree but a kind of yucca plant.

Joshua Tree is a dark-sky park, which means there are spectacular opportunities to view the star-studded night sky, particularly in the northern and eastern parts. As the main part of the park doesn't close at night, visitors can simply drive in and park to marvel at the Milky Way. There is also an observatory, but either way, an early arrival means spectacular red-coloured sunsets can be enjoyed, too.

PROJECT CREDITS

THE CHARMERS

BUSHY SUMMERS MINER'S SHACK (PP. 10–23) is a restored heritage miner's hut on the waterfront of a bay in Macquarie Harbour, Lettes Bay, Tasmania, Australia. Owners Claire Lloyd and Matthew Usmar Lauder normally live in Sydney, Australia, or Lesbos, Greece. Claire is a creative director and designer (clairelloyd.com). **e** office@clairelloyd.com **i** @bushysummers **w** (for rental) bushysummers.com **photography** Karina Camenzind (p. 12); Claire Lloyd (pp. 8 top left, 10, 15, 18, 20, 21 top left and bottom left); Estella Mason (pp. 11, 14, 16, 17, 19, 21 top right and bottom right, 22–23)

LOVE & MUTINY BEACH SHACK (PP. 24–35) is a restored midcentury fisherman's fibro beach shack on a tidal beachfront, surrounded by coastal scrub, in Chinaman Wells, Yorke Peninsula, South Australia. Owners Emma Read and Sarah Hall normally live in Willunga, South Australia. Emma and Sarah are interior design/stylists. **e** stay@loveandmutiny.com.au; hello@readandhall.com.au; **i** @loveandmutiny **w** (for rental) readandhall.com.au; loveandmutiny.com.au **photography** Hannah Puechmarin (hannahpuechmarin.com; pp. 8 top middle, 24–33); takeus_withyou (front cover); Jason Watson (pp. 34–35)

WILD SURF CABIN (PP. 36–51) is a restored shingled fisherman's cottage on a sea coast in Nova Scotia, Canada. Owners Catherine Bernier and Gabriel Denis are originally from Quebec and moved to Nova Scotia. Catherine is a freelance writer and photographer; her studio is The Parcelles (@theparcelles) and she also works at *BESIDE* magazine (beside.media). **e** catherinebernierda@gmail.com **i** @cath.be; @gabdenis **photography** Catherine Bernier (pp. 2–3, 8 top right, 36–40, 41 right, 42–49, back cover top right); Emma Duchaine (p. 41 left); Shutterstock/njene (pp. 50–51)

VILLA SYSMÄ (PP. 52–65) is a newly built charcoal-painted wood cabin with an annex in a forest near Lake Päijänne, Sysmä, Finland. Owners Johanna Haltia and Mikko Haltia live here with their two sons, Luka (twelve) and Patrik (fourteen)—from Johanna's previous marriage—and Sofia (five). They normally live in Helsinki. Johanna is CEO of a fashion centre in Helsinki. **e** johanna.haltia@gmail.com; **i** @villasysma **photography** Johanna Haltia (pp. 8 middle left, 52–63); Shutterstock/Tummataika Photography (pp. 64–65)

THE BOOKWORM CABIN (PP. 66–75) is an architect-designed ash-grey cabin in a pine woodland in Adelin, Mazovia, Poland. Owners Bartłomiej Kraciuk and Marta Puchalska-Kraciuk, with their two young children, normally live in Warsaw. Bartłomiej is a hospitality entrepreneur and Marta is an interior design architect at Moszczyńska Puchalska (moszczynskapuchalska.com). For this project, she adapted an original cabin design by Pole Architekci, but installed her own interior design. **e** book@bookwormcabin.xyz; **i** @bookwormcabin **w** (for rental) bookwormcabin.xyz **photography** Piotr Bednarski (pp. 8 middle right, 66–72); Shutterstock/ArtMediaFactory (pp. 74–75)

VINTERSPARV COTTAGE (PP. 76–87) is a traditional *röd stuga* (red country cottage) or *sommarhus* (summer house) in the countryside near a lake, forests and some farmland in Tisselskog, Dalsland, Sweden. Owners Linnea Klingström and Gustav Klingström and their two children, daughter Ingrid and son Arvid, and two cats, normally live in Gothenburg. **e** vintersparv@hotmail.com; linnea.a@outlook.com **i** @vintersparv **photography** Linnea Klingström (pp. 8 bottom left, 76–85); Shutterstock/UllrichG (pp. 86–87)

THE NENE NEST (PP. 88–99) is a renovated sugar plantation cottage a few steps from Kekaha Beach, Kauai, Hawaii, United States. Owners Melissa Lipe and Kyle Lipe and their two children, Madelyn (nine) and Henry (six), normally live in Seattle. Melissa has an interest in interior design. **e** melissa.lipe@gmail.com; **i** @thenenenest.kauai **w** (for rental) thenenenestkauai.com **photography** Julia Kathleen (juliakathleenphoto .com; pp. 89, 92 bottom left); Shutterstock/Shane Myers Photography (pp. 98–99); Surf + Pine (surfandpine.com, @colorsofspring; pp. 8 bottom middle, 88, 90, 91, 92 top left and right, and bottom right, 93, 94, 95, 96, 97)

HEMLOCK HOLLOW A-FRAME (PP. 100–113) is a renovated A-frame in a mountain forest near a river in the Pocono Mountains, Pennsylvania, United States. Owners Lauren Spear and Michael Goesele, and their dog, Bernie, normally live in New York City. Lauren (laurenwesleyspear .com) is an architectural designer, and Michael (michaelgoesele.com) is a creative director. **e** lauren.wesley.spear@gmail.com; info@ michaelgoesele.com; **i** @thehemlockhollow; @_el_wesley_; @mgoesele; **w** (for rental) airbnb .com/h/thehighlandbungalow (Note: Hemlock Hollow was not available for rent at time of press, but it may be added to their other listing later.) **photography** Natalie Chitwood (nataliechitwood .com; @natchitwood; pp. 100, 103, 104, 105, 106–7, 108, 111); Michael Goesele and Lauren Spear (pp. 8 bottom right, 101, 102, 109, 110); Shutterstock/Rabbitti (pp. 112–13)

THE MODERNS

BAKER BOYS BEACH HOUSE (PP. 116–27) is an award-winning contemporary black beach house set high in bush overlooking the beach on North Stradbroke Island, Queensland, Australia. The owners, Vicki Dubois and Frederic Dubois (with their son, Olle/Oliver) normally live in Brisbane. Architects Monika Obrist and Erhard Rathmayr (creative director at Refresh Design) designed the home. The interior design was by Vicki (Flokk Interiors) and construction was by Frederic (Bespoke Constructions). **e** vicki@flokkinteriors.com.au; fred@bespokeconstructions.com.au **i** @refreshdesign; **w** bespokeconstructions.com.au; flokkinteriors.com.au; refreshdesign.com.au **photography** Frederic Dubois (p. 125); Christopher Frederick Jones (studio@cfjphoto .com.au; pp. 114 top left, 116, 118–19, 120, 122–23); Ryan Renshaw (p. 117); Shutterstock/bru greg (pp. 126–27)

HALFMOON BAY CABIN (PP. 128–41) is a contemporary black cabin set in the forest overlooking Halfmoon Bay, British Columbia, Canada. Owners Patrick Warren and Kevin Kaufman, and their dog, Taavi, normally live in Vancouver. Patrick is a senior associate and business partner at Frits de Vries Architects + Associates, and Kevin is a marine biologist. **e** patrick@frits.ca; **i** @fdvarch; **w** https://frits.ca/ project/halfmoon-bay-cabin; frits.ca **photography** Love Tree Photography (p. 129); Ema Peter (pp. 114 top middle, 128, 130, 132–33, 134, 135, 137, 138, 139); Shutterstock/Wirestock Creators (pp. 140–41)

CASA SALVAJE (PP. 142–55) is a brutalist off-grid house set in mountains in a cloud forest in Palmichal de Acosta, Costa Rica. Owners Lilly Peña and her young adult children, Camille, Stephan, and Natalia, and dogs, normally live in San José. Lilly is a documentary film maker and founder of Mercado KM0 (km0mercado@gmail .com), an organic farmers and green products market in San José. Architect: María de la Paz Alice, founder of Mazpazz Arquitectura (**e** mapaz@zurcherarqui tectos.com; **i** @mazpazz_arquitectura) **photography** Andrés García Lachner (pp. 114 top right, 146, 147, 149, 150–51, 153, 154–55); Matias Sauter Morera (pp. 142, 143, 144–45, 152, back cover top left)

CASITA JABIN (PP. 156–63) is a modern pink cube set in the jungle in Valladolid, Yucatán, Mexico. Owners Anette Urbina Gamboa and Eduardo De la Peña Corral, with their baby daughter, Isabella, normally live in Mexico City.
e annetteug219@gmail.com; **i** @casitajabin
w (for rental) airbnb.com/h/casitajabin
Architect: TACO architects (**e** info@arquitectura contextual.com; **w** arquitecturacontextual.com)
photography Leo Espinosa (pp. 114 middle left, 156, 158, 160, 161); Shutterstock/Simon Dannhauer (pp. 162–63); Anette Urbina Gamboa (p. 157)

KAWAU ISLAND BACH (PP. 164–73) is a modern polycarbonate and corrugated-iron-clad structure (inspired by the humble boat shed) on the shoreline of Harris Bay, Kawau Island, Hauraki Gulf, New Zealand. Owners Greg Knowles and Dr Alison Knowles normally live in Auckland.
Architect: Crosson Architects (**w** crosson.co.nz; **i** @crossonarchitects)
photography Greg and Alison Knowles (pp. 165, 171); Jude Wood (pp. 172–73); David Straight (pp. 114 middle right, 164, 166, 167, 168, 169, 170)

USETT HYTTE (PP. 174–85) is a contemporary wooden chalet set on a snowy hill in the ski fields of Sjusjøen, Ringsaker, Norway. Owners Marianne and Jon Vigtel Hølland and teen children, Jesper and Ylva, plus dogs, normally live in Oslo. Marianne is a designer with a 'slow design' philosophy, and she's known for her 'wild knitting' and textiles.
e marianne@slowdesign.no; **i** @slow_design
w slowdesign.no
Architect: Benedicte Sund-Mathisen of Suma Arkitektur (**e** benedicte@sumaarkitektur.no; **w** sumaarkitektur.no)
photography Marianne Vigtel Hølland (Slow Design Studio; pp. 114 bottom left, 174, 175, 177, 178, 178, 179, 180, 181, 182, 183, 184–85, back cover bottom left)

SOL TO SOUL HOUSE (PP. 186–97) is a white prefab house set in the high desert among boulders in Pioneertown, California, United States. Owners Leslie Longworth and teens, son Harrison and daughter Lucie, normally live in Los Angeles. Leslie is a writer, creator and investor.
e leslielongworth@gmail.com
i @soltosoulhouse
w (for rental) soltosoulhouse.com
Architect: Cover (**e** hello@buildcover.com; **w** buildcover.com)
photography Melissa Gidney Daly (@melissagidneyphoto; @suro_living; pp. 114 bottom middle, 186, 191, 192 top left and bottom right; 194 middle and right); Leslie Longworth (p. 187); Minh T (@ThisMintyMoment; p. 193); Phil Nguyen (@philngyn; pp. 188–99, 190); Chris Poplawski (@chrisroams; pp. 194 left, 196–97, back cover bottom right); Meir Schonbrun (@meirr; pp. 192 top right and bottom left, 195)

HACHI LILY BUNGALOW (PP. 198–207) is a bungalow-style dwelling in a pomelo grove (bordered by a water lily pond) in Thủy Biều, Hue, Vietnam. Owner Nguyen Khanh Van normally lives in Hue city.
Architect: Nguyen Huu Son Duong (SILAA Architects; **e** contact@silaaarchitects.com; **i** @silaa.architects; #hachililyhouse)
photography Hoang Le Photographer (hoang814 .tumblr.com; pp. 114 bottom right, 198, 200, 201, 202–3, 204, 205); courtesy SILAA Architects (p. 199); Shutterstock/Nguyen Thai Vinh (pp. 206–7)

THE RUSTICS

LA FERMETTE DU MERLE (PP. 210–19) is a nineteenth-century farmhouse set in undulating farmland with views of Le Morvan forest in Crux-la-Ville, Burgundy, France. Owners Morgane van Liere and Arvid Niemeijer, with baby Mathieu, normally live in Hilversum, the Netherlands. Morgane is a brand manager/marketer with an interest in interior design.
e info@lafermettedumerle.fr; **i** @fermette_dumerle; **w** (for rental) lafermettedumerle.fr
photography Morgane van Liere (pp. 208 top left, 210–17); Shutterstock/Anton Havelaar (pp. 218–19)

AGAPAKI STUDIO (PP. 220–31) is a small studio on a rocky hilltop in the ancient village of Agapi, Tinos, Greece. Owners Alexandra Papadimouli and Peter Grivas normally live in Athens. Alexandra is an artist specialising in artworks inspired by Greek island life, with a special focus on the Cyclades.
e info@theroundbutton.com
i @to_agapaki_tinos; @theroundbutton
w theroundbutton.com
photography Alexandra Papadimouli (pp. 208 top right, 220–29); Shutterstock/RedHeadAnnika (pp. 230–31)

TRULLO STELLA MARE (PP. 232–43) is a historic *trullo*, a traditional Apulian dry-stone hut with conical roofs, set amid olive groves in Lamie di Olimpia, Puglia, Italy. Owners Paola Totaro and Robert Wainwright normally live in London. Paola is an author and award-winning news reporter, specialising in international current affairs, politics and travel. Robert, also a journalist and prize-winning Australian author, has had fourteen books published. Both recently published the book *On the Scent* (London: Elliott&Thompson, 2022).
e paolatotaro60@gmail.com; **i** @aggiornalista
w (for rental) paolatotaro.com/trulli-madly-deeply; rental *United Kingdom* essentialitaly.co.uk/puglia/villas/trullo-stella-mare; *Italy* trullionline.com/struttura/trullo-stella-mare
blog trullimadlydeeply.blogspot.com
photography Shutterstock/ecstk22 (pp. 242–43); Paola Totaro (pp. 208 middle left, 232–41)

YUI VALLEY KOMINKA (PP. 244–53) is an old wooded *kominka* (a traditional wooden country house) set in the hills (full of bamboo forests and green tea plantations) of Tamatori, Fujieda, Shizuoka, Japan. Owners Hila Gay Kajiyama and Daisuke Kajiyama usually go back and forth to Israel, but have stayed in Japan due to COVID-19.
e haleluya.bamboo@gmail.com; **i** @yui_valley
w (for rental) yuivalley.com
photography Daisuke Kajiyama (pp. 208 middle centre, 244, 247, 248–49, 250 bottom left, 251 bottom left); Hila Gay Kajiyama (pp. 245, 250 top and bottom right, 251 top and bottom right, 252–53)

FINCA ALFABIA (PP. 254–63) is a three-hundred-year-old *finca* (traditional farmhouse) in olive groves in the centre of the island, in Ruberts, Mallorca, Spain. Owners Tatiana Baibabaeva and Tyson Strang, with their son Ferrán, normally live in New York City. Tyson and Tatiana are the founders of the interior design team Terra Coll Home and are both ceramicists, who formerly worked in education and fashion, respectively.
e terracollhome@gmail.com; **i** @terracollhome; @baibabaeva; **w** terracollhome.com
photography Olaf Tausch (pp. 262–63); Terra Coll Home (pp. 208 middle right, 254–61)

LITTLE HARP COTTAGE (PP. 264–71) is a seventeenth-century white stone cottage set in the rolling hills of the ancient hamlet Old Radnor, Powys, Wales, United Kingdom. Owners Albert Hill and Ciara Hill, with their two children, Arlo and Jackson, and dog, Rusty, normally live in Surrey, England. Albert Hill is the cofounder of themodernhouse.com and inigo.com, and former design editor with *Wallpaper**.
e welcome@littleharp.co.uk; **i** @littleharp.co.uk
w (for rental) littleharp.co.uk
photography Ben Draguisky (p. 267 top left); Albert Hill (p. 265); themodernhouse.com (pp. 208 bottom left, 264, 266, 267 top right, and bottom left and right, 269); Shutterstock/William Perugini (pp. 270–71)

DESERT CABIN (PP. 272–83) is a boho white masonry cabin set in the desert in Joshua Tree, California, United States. Owners Kathrin Smirke and Brian Smirke normally live with their cat, Cobie, on the Mendocino coast, California, United States. Kathrin is a designer and stained-glass artist, and Brian is a musician and real estate developer.
e kathrin@weareinourelement.com
i @cabincabincabin; @kathrinsmirke; @briansmirke; @weareinourelement
w (for rental) weareinourelement.com
photography Shutterstock/Dennis Silvas (pp. 282–83); Brian Smirke (pp. 208 bottom right, 272, 274–75, 276, 277, 278, 279 top and bottom left, 280, 281); Kathrin Smirke (273, 279 bottom right)

Susan Redman is a journalist and editor with a passion for architecture and design. This has led to an extraordinary career writing about homes, and the people who design, decorate and live in them. She has worked as a design columnist for the *Sydney Morning Herald*, the *Age*, *Vogue Australia*, and the *Japan Times*, and has been a regular contributor to various home, fashion and lifestyle publications and magazines (print and digital), including *Country Style*, *Home Beautiful*, *Vogue Living*, *Belle*, *Gardening Australia*, plus Houzz and Domain. She also writes about art, travel, and pop culture, and authored *My Dream Kombi*, a book which celebrates the retro design icon and the fascinating stories of the surfies, hippies and celebrities who travelled in them.

Published in Australia in 2022 by
The Images Publishing Group Pty Ltd
ABN 89 059 734 431

Offices

MELBOURNE

Waterman Business Centre
Suite 64, Level 2 UL40
1341 Dandenong Road
Chadstone, Victoria 3148
Australia
Tel: +61 3 8564 8122

NEW YORK

6 West 18th Street 4B
New York, NY 10011
United States
Tel: +1 212 645 1111

SHANGHAI

6F, Building C, 838 Guangji Road
Hongkou District, Shanghai 200434
China
Tel: +86 021 31260822

books@imagespublishing.com
www.imagespublishing.com

 A catalogue record for this book is available from the National Library of Australia

| Title: | Love Shacks: Romantic cabin charmers, modern getaways and rustic retreats around the world // Susan Redman |
| ISBN: | 9781864709339 |

This title was commissioned in IMAGES' Melbourne office and produced as follows: EDITORIAL Georgia (Gina) Tsarouhas, ART DIRECTION/PRODUCTION Nicole Boehringer, with thanks to Rosy Apicella. Editorial concept and direction: Susan Redman with Mark Ryan.

Printed on 150gsm GalerieArt Natural paper by DZS Grafik (Slovenia)